PS (Phosphatidylserine)

Nature's Brain Booster
For Memory, Mood, and Stress

A Vital Lipid Nutrient For
Total Health Management

Parris M. Kidd, PhD

Total Health Management Series No. 1

A *totalhealth* Publication
Published by Total Health Communications, Inc.
165 N. 100 East, Suite 2
St. George, Utah 84770
Tel: 435.673.1789
Fax: 435.634.9336
www.totalhealthmagazine

Printed in the United States of America

Total Health Management Series No. 1

First printing, November 2005

ISBN 0-9774232-0-4

10 9 8 7 6 5 4 3 2 1

First Edition

Foreword

It is a distinct privilege to introduce "PS (PhosphatidylSerine), Nature's Brain Booster," the first in a series of Total Health Management publications. As publisher of *totalhealth* magazine I have had the opportunity to work closely over the past ten years with Dr. Parris Kidd and Mr. Peter Rohde on their journey to create an awareness of the scientifically proven properties of this amazing nutritional ingredient, and in educating healthcare professionals, the health food industry, and consumer markets. Mr. Rohde developed consumer awareness of PS through educational marketing. He generously sponsored research to verify its clinical benefits.

As an individual I have experienced the benefits of PS nearly every day for ten years, as well as observed its impact on the lives of family and friends, and even on an eleven year old pet who was brought back from severe dementia to reconnect with our family for the last two years of his life.

I am confident you will find the following information concerning the research-proven health benefits of PhosphatidylSerine (PS) a valuable, even critical, asset to maximizing your own mental acuity and prolonging the onset of or even reversing mental decline, as well as an excellent tool in dealing with physical, mental, emotional, and job-related stress. Also, PS is safe, non-addictive, and without debilitating, life threatening side effects.

Author Dr. Parris Kidd is recognized as the leading expert on the benefits of PS. He is internationally recognized as a researcher and scientist, and is widely sought after as a speaker and educator by both the health food industry and healthcare practitioner audiences.

For the past ten years, Dr. Kidd has been an associate editor and science advisor to *totalhealth* magazine. He has been our mentor, sounding board, and good friend. Over that period Dr. Kidd has contributed more than forty major articles covering a number of subjects critical to establishing and maintaining a healthy mind and body, as well as educating us to the benefits of nutritional supplementation and a total health management approach to potentiating our immune system and as therapy and co-therapy in combating disease.

In May of 1997 Dr. Kidd introduced the readers of *totalhealth* magazine to PS. His article generated an unprecedented response from our audience and initiated my continuing love affair with this magnificent dietary supplement, which I have taken nearly every day for the past ten years. The article also stressed the imperative of a total health management program to prolonging the onset of dementia, slowing its progression, and even reversing its severity. In October 2000 Dr. Kidd again reported on the overwhelming success of a study which incorporated PS and a total health management program as a safe and effective alternative to Ritalin with children experiencing ADHD, Attention Deficit Hperactivity Disorder.

Today, 57 years after the PS molecule was first isolated for chemical experimentation, hundreds of studies have been conducted on its pertinent benefits to our health. Of these, at least 21 have been double blind clinical trials with a consensus from the trials indicating PS benefits practically all of the brain's higher functions.

For the past eighteen years Dr. Kidd and Mr. Rohde have been instrumental in supervising and participating in the science necessary to identify and corroborate the health benefits of PS and other vital lipids, as well as to ensure the quality of the raw materials to be marketed for human consumption.

In 1994 PS was introduced to the American consumer. Today PS can be found on retail shelves nationwide and is widely recognized for its proven ability to help maintain and improve cognitive function in mature and aging adults, to help relieve stress and fatigue and elevate mood, as therapy for Attention Deficit Disorder in children, and for Alzheimer's disease.

There is no question PS should be lauded for its benefits to the human condition alone. However, I submit one more thought for your consideration. In his introduction beginning on page *xi*, Dr. Dharma Singh Khalsa relates that the incidence of Alzheimer's in our population will catapult from the current figure of 4.5 million individuals to over 16 million by 2015–2020. He also informs us that if we can delay the occurrence of symptoms for only five years, current thinking tells us, then we can reduce the incidence of Alzheimer's by 50 percent.

By current estimates this means a savings of one trillion dollars a year would be achieved.

Can PS alone do the job? Not necessarily. Can it play a major role? You bet.

Thank you for your interest in this publication. We are currently in the process of producing the second Total Health Management publication on GPC (GlyceroPhosphoCholine) which will be available in 2006.

In Good Health,

Lyle Hurd

ABOUT THE AUTHOR

Internationally recognized nutrition scientist Parris M. Kidd, PhD received the BSc (Zoology) First Class Honors degree at the University of the West Indies in Kingston, Jamaica, and the Ph.D. in Zoology-Cell Biology at the University of California at Berkeley. His PhD thesis explored cell membranes in the fertilization process, and his current work with phospholipid nutrients further extends this interest since phospholipids are major building blocks for the membranes of all cells. Dr. Kidd has been educating the professional and lay public about PhosphatidylSerine (PS) and other phospholipids since 1987.

AUTHOR ACKNOWLEDGMENTS

I am grateful to Mr. Peter Rohde for the opportunity to intellectually collaborate with him since 1987, for his partnership in developing and popularizing phospholipid products, and for his generous financial sponsorship for my phospholipid work.

I thank Mr. Lyle Hurd for encouraging me to write for the public, for graciously granting me access to *totalhealth* magazine, and for supporting the Total Health Management series. I am indebted to Katherine Owens for the text design and typography of this book and for many other contributions to making it real.

Dr. Dharma Singh Khalsa, Dr. Thomas Crook III, and numerous other colleagues offered constructive critiques that have enriched this text. Any inaccuracies or misstatements that remain are solely the responsibility of the author.

Contents

FOREWORD by Lyle Hurd, Publisher *iii*

ABOUT THE AUTHOR; ACKNOWLEDGEMENTS *v*

GLOSSARY OF TECHNICAL TERMS *ix*

INTRODUCTION by Dharma Singh Khalsa, M.D. *xi*

1 PS, VITAL LIPID™ AND PREMIER BRAIN NUTRIENT 1
The Clinically Proven Benefits of PS
A Safe and Effective Orthomolecular Supplement
A Vital Lipid for Nerve Cells
PS and Total Health Management Build Brain Power

2 PS MAY REVERSE EARLY BRAIN DECLINE 11
Crook's Team Advances Practical Cognition Testing
Age Associated Memory Impairment Signals Decline
PS Helps Revitalize the Declining Brain

3 USEFUL TOOL AGAINST SEVERE MEMORY LOSS 21
Abnormal Memory Decline Can Lead to Dementia
Dementia as Daily Existence
Total Health Management Can Delay Dementia
The Matrix of Risk Factors for Dementia
PS Double Blind Trials Show Benefit Against Dementia

4 LIFTING DEPRESSION AND ANXIETY 31
Trials With PS for Depression and Anxiety
PS Mood Benefits Are Likely Based in Membranes

5 DISARMING MENTAL STRESS, A MEMORY KILLER 35
Fight or Flight: Good Thing That Can Go Bad
PS Helps Students Manage Mental Stress
PS Revitalizes the Stress Response in the Elderly
PS Partially Rejuvenates Aging Brain Rhythms

6 PS ALSO HELPS MANAGE PHYSICAL STRESS   43
PS Improves Physical Stress Management in Students
PS Improves Stress Hormone Status
PS Helps Avoid "Overtraining" During Workouts

7 PS FOR "ADD"—EXCELLENT EARLY RESULTS   47
The Kunin-Kidd Pilot Study
The Ryser-Kidd ADHD Case Series
Nutrients Are Safer Than Ritalin® for ADHD

8 PS AND DHA AMPLIFY EACH OTHER'S BENEFITS   53
Two Overlapping Building Blocks for Cell Membranes
Omega-3 Fatty Acids, Important For the Entire Body
DHA, the Omega-3, Very Important for Brain Cells
PS and DHA Combine to Optimize Brain Function

9 PS FOR TOTAL HEALTH MANAGEMENT   59
PS is Safe to Take and Very Well Tolerated
How to Take PS for Best Results
Total Health Management Will Amplify PS Benefits
The Top Ten Practices of Total Health Management

10 PS DOES SOMETHING FOR EVERYONE   67
PS Really Can Revitalize the Brain
Taking a Stand for Dementia Prevention: Dr. Dharma
PS Can Benefit Other Brain Conditions
Parting Message: Everyone May Benefit from PS

APPENDIX: DOUBLE BLIND TRIALS   73
Trials Against Age-Associated Memory Impairment
Trials Against Alzheimer's Dementia
Trials Against Non-Alzheimer's Dementia

RESOURCES   79

SCIENTIFIC REFERENCES CITED IN THE TEXT   81

Glossary of Technical Terms

PS
Abbreviation for PhosphatidylSerine

PhosphatidylSerine (abbr. PS)
Pronounced *fos-fa-tie-dil-see-reen*. A phospholipid substance present in all human and other known cells. Found in small amounts in common foods.

Total Health Management™
A personal approach to health that takes into account all the factors that positively or negatively impact health. Requires a commitment to self-education and proactive intervention as necessary to maintain or pursue a very high level of health.

Nutrient
A substance coming from foods that helps the body stay alive.

Vital Lipid™
Fat-soluble substance vital for health. Phospholipids, essential fatty acids, cholesterol, and the fat-soluble vitamins, all are vital lipids.

Fats
Storage forms of lipids, distinctly different from phospholipids.

Phospholipid
Pronounced *fos-fo-lip-id*. A class of substances with molecular design suitable to make cell membranes. PS is a phospholipid.

Orthomolecule
Literally, a molecule orthodox to the body. A substance naturally part of human biochemistry and found in all the body's cells and tissues.

Protein
A catalytic molecule assembled from amino acids. Proteins of cell membranes interact with phospholipids for optimal function.

Membrane (cell membrane)
A very thin but continuous, uninterrupted sheet of biological molecules. A double molecular layer of lipids (the "bilayer") houses catalytic protein molecules.

Cell
The basic unit of independent life.

Memory
The ability to revisit an earlier experience.

Cognition
Collective term for the variety of sophisticated brain functions that

endow humans with reasoning power. Memory, learning, comprehension, attention, concentration, all are cognitive abilities.

AAMI
Age-associated memory impairment. Diagnosed in people over age 50. Memory capacity is worse than two-thirds (67 percent) of young adults.

ARCD
Age-related cognitive decline. Cognitive function is worse than two thirds (67 percent) of people in the same age group.

MCI
Mild cognitive impairment. Impaired memory with other cognitive functions intact. People with this condition are at high risk for dementia.

Dementia
Loss of mental capacity and the capacity to reason, so severe that social and occupational functioning is markedly impaired.

Depression
State of negative mood. If prolonged over time, can become *clinical* or *major* depression.

Anxiety
State of excessive concern over life issues.

Transmitter (Nerve transmitter)
A substance released by a nerve cell to influence the activity of another nerve cell or a different cell type, a muscle fiber for example.

MRI, SPECT, PET
Abbreviations for Magnetic Resonance Imaging, Single-Photon Emission Computed Tomography, and Positron Emission Tomography. These imaging techniques produce useful information on the intact brain.

EEG (ElectroEncephaloGraphy)
An early "non-invasive" method to measure brain electrical activity.

Vitamin
A substance required by the body for normal function, and the absence of which results in poor health (a vitamin deficiency state). Many vitamins cannot be made by the body and must come from the diet.

Stress
Challenge to the body's ongoing efforts to stay healthy (homeostasis).

Stressor
Any agent that exerts stress on the body. Can be emotional, chemical, physical, vibrational. All stressors contribute to ill-health and risk of brain deterioration.

Introduction

For over a decade I've known Dr. Parris Kidd as a first class nutritional scientist and educator, now with over 20 years of experience in designing nutritional products and in educating the public and physicians about their use. In my professional medical opinion, he is the world's leading authority on the use of PhosphatidylSerine (PS), a well proven compound to maximize mental function as well as prevent and even reverse memory loss. Because of my longstanding personal friendship and professional relationship with Dr. Kidd, I was delighted when he asked me to write an introduction for his new book.

One of the biggest problems I see here in America is the rapid increase in the number of people expected to develop Alzheimer's disease in the next 10–15 years. Because of the aging of the population, the number of people who will have this catastrophic mind-robbing and financially draining illness is predicted to skyrocket from the current 4.5 million to over 16 million by 2015–2020.

There is hope, however. Emerging science, including work done by Dr. Kidd, the Alzheimer's Prevention Foundation, of which I'm president and medical director, and others at the highest level of academic medicine, has shown that it may be possible to prevent Alzheimer's disease or at least to delay its development.

What we now know is that Alzheimer's disease is a problem that doesn't occur overnight. It takes as long as 30 years to manifest. If we can delay the occurrence of symptoms for only five years, current thinking tells us that then we can reduce the incidence of Alzheimer's by 50 percent. And if we can delay it by 10 years, which I believe is entirely possible, we can virtually eliminate it; people will simply pass away before they develop Alzheimer's.

There is no magic bullet drug or even nutrient that will make the prevention of Alzheimer's a reality. It takes a total health approach. What does that involve? It includes four steps: eating well and taking supplements, managing stress, getting adequate physical, mental and mind/body exercise, and considering medicines and hormone replacement therapy when needed.

PhosphatidylSerine and the other compounds Dr. Kidd tells us about in this new book plays a very important role in that lifestyle approach. In my clinical experience, PS is very effective at reversing signs of memory loss such as the inability to recall names, numbers, faces and other manifestations of what I call Swiss cheese memory. Swiss cheese memory is when your thoughts seem to vanish; they fall down a hole in your mind. When you take PhosphatidylSerine, it's like having a safety net in your head;

words, names and thoughts seem to bounce right back into your brain and onto your tongue. It's actually quite remarkable.

One patient of mine, an attorney from Washington D.C., noticed an improvement in his brain power almost immediately. For others, it may take three months to work. But regardless, if takes one day or three months, it's worth the wait.

It's good for your brain to learn new things, and I did learn something new from reading this book. PhosphatidylSerine is also effective in helping reverse symptoms of Attention Deficit Disorder in children without the use of amphetamine-like stimulant drugs such as Ritalin. Beyond that, PhosphatidylSerine helps you recover faster when you exercise on a regular basis because it blocks the weakening effects the stress hormone cortisol has on your muscles.

Here is my prescription for you: Relax in your favorite easy chair and enjoy this user friendly monograph about the hows and whys of a very important memory specific nutrient called PhosphatidylSerine, or PS. I know you won't be disappointed.

Dharma Singh Khalsa, M.D.
President/Medical Director
Alzheimer's Prevention Foundation
Author of *The Better Memory Kit*

To learn more about the work of Dharma Singh Khalsa, M.D., log onto www.drdharma.com.

To learn more about the work of the Alzheimer's Prevention Foundation log onto www.Alzheimersprevention.org.

CHAPTER 1

PS, Vital Lipid™ and Premier Brain Nutrient

P hosphatidylSerine or PS (pronounced *fos-fa-tie-dil-see-reen*) is a biological substance that occurs naturally throughout the human body. PS has a unique molecular structure that makes it a building block for all the cells of the body. When added to the daily diet as a supplemental nutrient concentrate, PS can have great benefits for the human brain.

The PS (PhosphatidylSerine) molecule

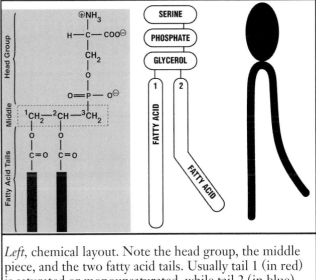

Left, chemical layout. Note the head group, the middle piece, and the two fatty acid tails. Usually tail 1 (in red) is saturated or monounsaturated, while tail 2 (in blue) typically is polyunsaturated. *Center and right*, symbolic representations as used in membrane diagrams.

- PS occurs naturally in all cells, and this may explain how it can be an extremely safe dietary supplement.
- PS is found mostly in the brain, and clinical trials show that supplementing the diet with PS improves a variety of brain functions.
- PS is lacking in the typical daily diet, and takes a lot of energy for the body to synthesize, making dietary supplementation a convenient and effective option.

PS (PhosphatidylSerine)

Chemically PS is a phospholipid, one of a unique group of substances that play many lifesaving roles in the body. PS and other phospholipids serve as cell membrane building blocks, lipoprotein building blocks, surface-active agents, emulsifiers, and as protein function regulators. The phospholipids (PL) are so essential to life that they have been called *vital lipids.*[2]

Technically, PS is not a vitamin because the body can make it from simpler substances (using processes of "bio-synthesis"). However, the energy it costs the body to "bio-synthesize" PS is quite high, making it more energy-effective to obtain PS as a nutrient from foods. The intake of PS from foods is quite low.

Plant foods supply very little PS, and animal foods (other than brain, not a common food) have only modest amounts, so that the total dietary intake of PS is in the range of 75–100 milligrams (mg) per day. This may explain why people can experience benefit from supplemental intakes of 100–300 mg per day. This amounts to a doubling of the daily intake of PS, at a minimum.

PS is more concentrated in the brain than in any other tissue of the body. The findings from controlled clinical trials suggest that when the dietary intake of PS is doubled or better still, quadrupled, through taking it as a dietary supplement, a majority of individuals derive measurable brain benefits. The modest supply of PS coming from the modern diet simply may not be adequate to support optimal brain function.

The PS molecule is involved in many aspects of human biochemistry. PS was first isolated for chemical examination in 1948, by Folch, and this breakthrough spurred research into its many life functions.[3] There are now thousands of research studies available on PS.[4]

Starting around the mid-1980s, through research trials with human volunteers, it quickly became evident that PS as a dietary supplement had highly positive benefits for a variety of higher brain functions. Among the functions benefited by PS were memory, learning, comprehension, word recall—all individual features of the brain performance spectrum called *cognition.* At this point PS has been investigated in a larger number of clinical trials and other controlled human studies than most pharmaceuticals have had.

Along with its measurable improvements to cognition, mood, anxiety, and coping with stress, PS improves many technical measures of brain activity. Take EEG, (ElectroEncephaloGraphy) for instance. From EEG studies it was found that PS can partially correct abnormal brain electrical activity, as sometimes seen in Parkinson's disease patients[5] and in epileptics.[6] These "normalizing" changes under the influence of PS would sometimes improve the patient's quality of life.

Then there were more modern results from brain imaging. Sophisticated imaging PET (Positron Emission Tomography) has established that PS can boost energy production throughout the brain.[7] The brain is so dependent on energy production that any means of improving its capacity to make energy offers promise for far-reaching improvements in function.

At the biochemical level, PS is found to improve numerous nerve transmitter systems in the human brain. PS is required for the packaging, release, and receptor actions of acetylcholine, serotonin, dopamine, epinephrine, norepinephrine, GABA, and other transmitters. Rather than simply raising transmitter levels in the brain tissue, PS improves their effectiveness fundamentally at the cell membrane level.

Acting through many different pathways, PS is clinically proven to benefit a diverse array of the subjects who took part in the many clinical trials.

The Clinically Proven Benefits of PS

PS as a brain nutrient is doubly positive, being highly efficacious AND having zero bad side effects. This sets PS apart from pharmaceuticals. After more than twenty years of extensive, controlled testing with human volunteers, with lab animals, and in other experimental systems, PS is confirmed to have a near-ideal "benefit-risk profile." This profile for PS is exceptional, not just against pharmaceuticals but also when compared to other nutrients.

The randomized, controlled, double blind clinical trial is the "gold standard" for medical assessment of a drug, nutrient, or medical device. Though the double blind trial has its limits, it is the most objective way to test whether an agent truly has human benefits. The meaning of double blind is that neither the researchers nor the human subjects knew which subjects were getting the most active treatment and which were not.

PS has been subjected to at least 21 double blind clinical trials. The consensus from these trials is that PS benefits practically all of the brain's higher functions. The clinical data accumulated from over twenty years' research substantiates that PS has the following clinical benefits:[8]

- PS improves memory, learning and other cognitive functions in people who are substantially impaired compared to others in their age group.

- PS can improve activities of daily living (ADL) and other quality of life, for people who suffer more severe memory loss.

- PS can improve negative mood (depression) and ease anxiety in young people as well as the elderly.

- PS can help individuals cope with stress, both physical and emotional.

- PS has the potential to help children with attention and behavior problems.

- PS as a dietary supplement is very well tolerated, with virtually no adverse effects.

PS is so well proven that even the skeptical Food and Drug Administration of the United States has allowed it to have two "qualified health claims" (see the box below).

FDA—APPROVED HEALTH CLAIMS FOR PS[9]

(Exact text as required by the FDA)

"Phosphatidylserine (PS) may reduce the risk of cognitive dysfunction in the elderly. Very limited and preliminary scientific research suggests that PS may reduce the risk of cognitive dysfunction in the elderly. FDA concludes that there is little scientific evidence supporting this claim."

"Phosphatidylserine (PS) may reduce the risk of dementia in the elderly. Very limited and preliminary scientific research suggests that PS may reduce the risk of dementia in the elderly. FDA concludes that there is little scientific evidence supporting this claim."

The overly cautious language for these claims, which FDA mandates can only be stated word for word, is at best a grudging concession to the extensive clinical research done with PS. Considering this agency's legendary toughness against dietary supplements, FDA's willingness to go this far with PS suggests that they must be sure it is safe to take; also, that they are unable to deny PS can improve human brain function.

A Safe and Effective Orthomolecular Supplement

Its near-ideal benefit-risk profile sets PS apart from the drugs approved for treating memory decline and from the many herbal extracts often touted as brain panaceas. Without doubt, its decades-old track record of exceptional safety is attributable to PS being an *orthomolecule*.

The term orthomolecule stands for molecule orthodox (familiar) to the body, as first defined in 1968 by the legendary two-time Nobel Laureate Linus Pauling. An orthomolecule is naturally and routinely part and parcel of the body's normal biochemistry.

The brilliant Professor Pauling had the vision that orthomolecules should be safe to take as dietary supplements precisely because they are biochemically familiar to the body. He also reasoned that their biochemical intimacy with human cells should give orthomolecules a metabolic advantage over substances that are not naturally a part of the body's biochemistry. Now, almost four decades after Pauling developed this hypothesis, his reasoning is vindicated: orthomolecules have proven safer and more effective than herbal extracts and other non-orthomolecules.

PS is an orthomolecule for all life forms, all the way back to the most primitive single cells that already existed more than three billion years ago. This position of PS is so different from the pharmaceuticals, almost all of which are chemicals foreign to the body and toxic to our tissues in varying degrees. Its superiority as an extensively tested orthomolecule makes PS a premier brain nutrient, a vital lipid for nerve cells.

A Vital Lipid for Nerve Cells

Biochemically, PS is a phospholipid *(fos-fo-lip-id)*.[8, 10] These lipid substances are distantly related to fatty lipids (triglycerides), which we know as *fats*. But in their function and their chemical structure, the phospholipids are very different lipids from fats.

The fat triglycerides are merely storage forms of lipid, the very material that we observe accumulating in our fat pads. The phospholipids are anything but storage fats: they are the main molecular building blocks for cell membranes, the dynamic structures upon which our cells rely for their functions. The phospholipids feed life dynamics at the cell level.

The phospholipids are used also to package up fats and transport them to the tissues. Phospholipids help the body to mobilize and utilize fats. The liver also uses phospholipids to make the bile fluid that aids in the digestion of our foods. All these are reasons why PS (and the other phospholipids) are appropriately called vital lipids.

Top: A schematic of a generalized animal cell showing the various membrane compartments that delineate organelles. *Bottom:* A stretch of cell membranes, showing proteins and other large molecules immersed in the matrix of phospholipids.

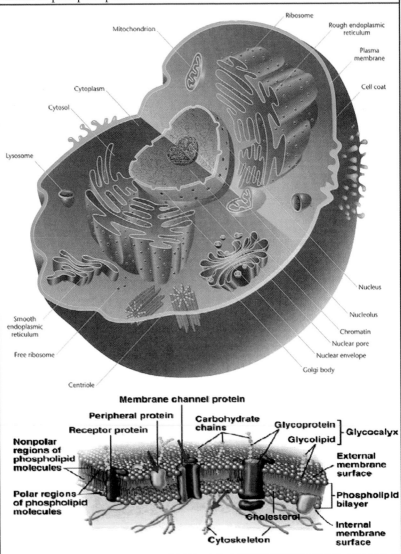

Cells are the most fundamental units of life. Our bodies are made up of trillions of cells. All cells have elaborate membrane systems, and from life's beginning PS and the other phospholipids were building blocks for the cells' membrane systems.

Cell membranes are continuous, unending sheets of biological molecules. They have a universal basic organization—a double layer of phospholipid molecules into which are inserted a small number of cholesterol and antioxidant molecules and catalytic proteins embedded in the phospholipid bilayer. This apparent simple organization of cell membranes actually is a functionally versatile, biochemically sophisticated, supra-molecular system responsible for the life essence of the cell. And the molecular

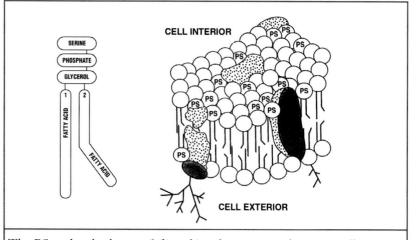

The PS molecular layout *(left)* and its placement in the outer cell membrane *(right)*. PS is preferentially located in the inner membrane half, and often enwraps key membrane proteins. ©Kidd PM, 1998.

organization of PS makes it very well suited as a unit building block for cell membranes.

All cells have PS in their membranes. Some have more PS than others, depending on their specialized functions. Nerve cells carry the most PS. They need ample PS in their membranes in order to generate electrical impulses and pass these impulses on to other cells. This is the essence of brain activity. Perhaps more than any other known biological molecule, PS in our nerve cells endows us with sophisticated brain power.

PS is also used in the body to facilitate other essential functions. PS is an essential player in the ongoing disposal of dead or dying cells.

PS (PhosphatidylSerine)

A healthy cell carries PS in the inner half of the outer cell membrane, with just about no PS in the outer half that faces the outer environment. Keeping PS in this membrane compartment requires constant expenditure of energy. A cell, as it becomes unhealthy, reaches a point where it can no longer muster sufficient energy to maintain this strict control over its membrane PS. The PS molecules then proceed to "flip" from the inside of the cell membrane to its outer face. As PS appears facing the outer environment, it serves as a kind of "flag" to alert roving immune cells that the cell is no longer healthy. This is the normal, routine means by which dead and dying cells are disposed of in the body.

PS also serves throughout the body as an essential component of the normal clotting processes that help stem blood loss following injury. It is also known to be involved in the "secretion" (release) of tiny membrane-bounded spherules ("vesicles") that bone cells secrete to make new bone. Secretion of many chemical transmitters and of many hormones occurs via similar mechanisms involving PS. In these many ways, the PS of our cell membranes helps us make the most efficient use of our life energy. Adequate availability of PS helps all our cells, tissues, and organs remain efficient, self-renewing, resistant to attack… able to stay healthy with the passing of time.

PS and Total Health Management™ Build Brain Power
The availability of PS as a safe, effective, and affordable brain nutrient comes just in time for a lot of people. Western society is in the grip of an epidemic of severe memory loss. At least two of every five people who reach 55 years of age have memory loss serious enough to be holding them back in their daily lives.[11,12] Anything that can be done to improve these cognitively challenged individuals would alleviate a great deal of anguish, not just for them but also for their families and communities. A further commitment to total health management would multiply their chances for breaking loose from this mental burden.

Taking PS is an excellent means toward long-term recovery of cognitive function (this doesn't usually happen overnight). Being so safe to take, PS can be used daily over a long period. It seems to have a regenerative type of effect, whatever the age of the individual. But PS cannot accomplish brain regeneration if nerve cells and circuits are being lost at too fast a rate. The rate of loss has to be slowed, and this is where daily practice of Total Health Management™ is the only real option—at least for the person who really wants to succeed.

In these modern times, with their harsh mental, physical, and chemical stress on the human body, implementing a lifestyle of Total Health Management (THM) is a means for the embattled individual to do as much as s/he can to hold off mental decline. THM offers the best means for us to maintain our brain power against the ravages of modern living. This is also good for the whole body; as the brain thrives, so also can the mind and spirit. As these thrive, so does the person as a whole.

Total Health Management is a self-help strategy for the personal pursuit of optimal health. THM, by definition, takes into account all the factors that can positively or negatively impact our health. THM works best when the individual makes a total commitment to lifelong health. Over the past decade this author and others have published on every facet of THM in the pages of *totalhealth* magazine.[13] Subsequent chapters will go deeper into the usefulness of PS for Total Health Management.

In the chapters that follow, the abundant scientific evidence on PS is reviewed and explained. It is my hope that this information will make PS more understandable and accessible for all who can benefit from it. That means all of us.

CHAPTER 2

PS May Reverse Early Brain Decline

- Brain decline that noticeably interferes with productivity and personal independence is not a normal feature of aging.
- A degree of brain decline abnormal for one's age group indicates increased risk for dementia later in life.
- Well-designed, randomized controlled clinical trials indicate PS can partially restore memory and other higher brain functions that have been lost. PS can revitalize the declining brain.

Conditions That Can Lead to Dementia

Dementia features severe decline in memory and at least one other aspect of cognition. Altogether, such deficits must be sufficiently severe to cause impairment in occupational or social functioning. Three conditions are recognized that can develop before the onset of dementia and signal increased risk for later development of dementia. These conditions are:

1. AGE-ASSOCIATED MEMORY IMPAIRMENT (AAMI). Common in individuals over age 50. AAMI individuals score in the bottom one-third when compared to young adults on standardized tests.[14] Risk for dementia is about three times that of non-AAMI people in the same over-50 age group.

2. AGE-RELATED COGNITIVE DECLINE (ARCD). Based on a more comprehensive evaluation than AAMI. ARCD individuals score in the bottom one-third for their own age group on standardized tests, rather than for young adults, which is the reference for AAMI. Therefore, people with ARCD are worse off than those with AAMI. About 10 percent worsen into dementia per year.[15]

3. MILD COGNITIVE IMPAIRMENT (MCI). These individuals have severely impaired memory while their other cognitive functions test normal. Not everyone with MCI will develop dementia, but some 10 to 15 percent of those with MCI progress to dementia each year.[16]

11

Many of us find that as we get into our forties or fifties, we're losing our mental edge. We lose things. It's become a hassle to keep track of our glasses and our keys (notice those huge key rings that some folks have, and the straps that keep their glasses on their necks). We can't remember the names of people we meet. Sometimes we even forget their faces. After reading something we quickly forget it.

We have trouble coming up with the right words—they're somewhere there but we can't find them. At the beginning we joke about it, but as it gets worse we move from being merely embarrassed to becoming really concerned.

We know something is wrong. Are we going to be an Alzheimer statistic? Some folks play down the problem by joking that they may have early Alzheimer's. It may not be Alzheimer's—yet. It could just be AAMI. Or ARCD. Or MCI. But all these are conditions that can progress to dementia (see box).

In recent years the direct imaging of brain function became a technological reality. Imaging generates pretty pictures that also have meaning. Functional brain imaging has revolutionized medical study of the brain and without any harm to the experimental subject.

The imaging of brain metabolism does not (so far) generate a precise estimate of the degree of dementia risk. But abnormally low brain function as reported from imaging is definitely a bad sign for the future and is a "wake-up call" for that individual. It's still a little early to say that poor brain metabolism means the person is likely to become demented, but certainly this person should be advised to clean up his or her life and get to work to rebuild his brain circuits.

Three imaging techniques monitor brain function: MRI (Magnetic Resonance Imaging), SPECT (Single-Photon Emission Computed Tomography), and PET (Positron Emission Tomography). (See the Resources section.) Imaging the suspicious brain can make a great difference because it enables early intervention to make positive changes. There likely is a "window of opportunity" for turning around brain decline, a period during which enough circuits are undamaged that they can produce or otherwise help replace the lost circuits. Past this point, the individual may not have sufficient remaining circuitry to adapt or to remain productive and live independently.

For the individual who notices he has problems and gets tested, then is confirmed as being at risk for dementia—what then? Better do something before it gets worse. But what can be done? Enter Dr. Tom Crook, one of the world's foremost memory researchers. By the time he got to PS, he had tested a great number of potential treatments for AAMI. After he and his international team of colleagues did two double blind trials on PS, they concluded that "PS is by far the best of all the drugs and nutritional supplements we have ever tested for retarding AAMI."

Crook's Team Advances Practical Cognition Testing[12, 17, 18]

Thomas Crook, Ph.D. has studied age-related memory loss since 1980. He has a distinguished scientific pedigree. After receiving his doctorate in psychology from the University of Maryland, he spent 14 years as a clinical researcher and research program director at the U.S. National Institute of Mental Health (NIMH). At various times he served as chairman of both the NIMH and the APA (American Psychological Association) task forces on diagnosis and treatment of memory decline.

Working at the U.S. Government's National Institute of Mental Health (NIMH), Dr. Crook soon led the field in the development of modern, convenient, and culturally relevant cognitive testing techniques. He put together a distinguished international team of researchers and together they worked to develop a new generation of tests that were easy to quantify yet provided solid data.

Dr. Crook and his team succeeded in moving beyond the traditional pencil and paper mental testing, with its burden of poor precision and notorious cultural bias. They developed interactive video testing that more directly measured how people applied their brain power to their daily lives.[12] After years of hard work, the outcome was a series of tests as follows:

➡ **First-last Names.** The subject is presented with a series of six pairs of first and last names, then given the last names and asked to pair them with the first names. This test also assesses verbal memory.

➡ **Name-face Recall.** Learning, immediate memory recall, and delayed memory recall (40 minutes later) of names presented together with faces on the video screen.

➡ **Face Recognition.** A good way to measure visual memory.

➡ **Grocery List Selective Reminding.** A list of 15 common grocery items is used to help assess verbal learning and delayed memory recall (after 40 minutes).

➡ **TELEPHONE DIALING.** Ability to memorize a telephone number, and keep it in memory while being delayed and distracted. In this test, performance of older subjects is more likely to be affected by distraction.

➡ **MISPLACED OBJECTS.** Placement and recall of keys, glasses, other common household objects within a computerized representation of a house. This test measures "verbal-visual associative" memory.

➡ **DIVIDED ATTENTION.** Measures reaction times related to simulated driving of a car, with radio weather and traffic reports as distractions while driving. Also measures recall of the announcements—"verbal-vocabulary" memory.

Left, the decline in memory for names with advancing age. Ability to recall a name 1 hour after hearing it—percent decline from age 25. *Right,* the decline in learning and remembering written information—percent decline from age 25.
Both from Crook and Adderly, *The Memory Cure.*[12]

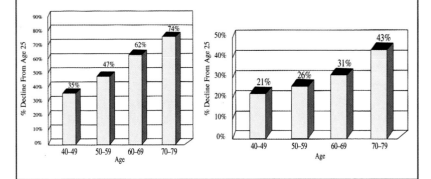

As simple as these tests are for the subject to take, they provide precise scores that help establish the boundaries between normal but age-related and disease-related cognitive performance in middle and late adulthood. They have an "everyday," common sense relevance that can be used by real people to get a real idea of how their higher mental functions are holding up against the passage of time.

Age-Associated Memory Impairment Signals Decline

Dr. Crook's group found that the decade by decade decline in name recall, name-face recall, learning and remembering written information, and several other cognitive functions they could measure, all were closely linked to aging. The most commonly reported problem, across the cultures they studied, was in remembering names. The figure shows that by age 60, well more than half of this capacity usually has been lost. By age 70 almost three-quarters of name recall capacity is lost. They also found that decline in the ability to learn and remember written information is less dramatic, but still worsens decade by decade and is almost half gone by age 70.

As they went on to spend years studying tens of thousands of people around the world, Dr. Crook's team made a key breakthrough. They found that the pattern of memory decline with age applies across cultures. They documented very similar data for decade by decade declines in the various cognitive functions, in Belgian and Italian subjects, in San Marino, in the United States, and in the Minangkabau people of Sumatra.

Using these culture-independent "baselines," Dr. Crook and his colleagues were able to conclude with confidence that whatever their cultural background, subjects who score statistically lower for their age group have AAMI, or Age-Associated Memory Impairment. Further, Crook's group could predict that this low-scoring group were at risk for catastrophic memory decline in later life.

The concept of AAMI was a major breakthrough by the NIMH work group chaired by Dr. Crook. Besides recognizing that those with AAMI who scored the worst were at risk for dementia, they also recognized that the AAMI diagnosis presented an opportunity to intervene early enough to possibly halt or at least slow any further decline. Dr. Crook and his colleagues were convinced that AAMI was a treatable condition. In contrast to people with dementia, people with AAMI were more likely to have enough brain circuitry to allow for some circuit rebuilding and hopefully, some partial recovery of lost function.

Technically, the term AAMI denotes people older than 50 years who report that their memory has declined since early adult life, who score in the lowest one-third compared to young adults (mid-twenties), and who have no medical or psychiatric conditions that could account for this loss. The AAMI diagnosis was adopted by both the American Psychiatric Association and the American Psychological Association. Both classify AAMI not as a disease but as a "developmental condition that merits attention and treatment."

Dr. Crook and his colleagues did precise testing of thousands of volunteers to develop accurate estimates of AAMI in the general population. They found that around 40 percent of people aged 50 to 59 qualified as AAMI, more than 50 percent of people aged 60 to 69, and an even greater proportion of those over 80. Between age 55 and age 85 the incidence of AAMI doubled (from 40 percent to 80 percent).

Their extensive test data strongly suggests that within the AAMI population, those individuals most measurably impaired by AAMI are likely to be at higher risk for developing Alzheimer's later in life. Though they are not demented, persons with more severe AAMI are likely to have major problems in coping with everyday life.

The recognition of AAMI as a treatable condition by Dr. Crook and others was a breakthrough toward early prevention of dementia. Progressive loss of the brain's higher functions brings considerable distress to the aging adult and to his loved ones. The body can go on for a long time after the mind is no longer useful. The only chance for avoiding this fate is to detect the problem and treat it as early as possible, before it can get worse.

People with AAMI can be quite badly impaired in their daily productivity and overall quality of life. They can develop fears that they have (or will get) Alzheimer's; often they become depressed or withdraw from their social circle. They can become afraid that deprived of their cognitive skills, they will be little more than vegetables. Serendipitously, the people in this population turned out to be the ones most likely to benefit from PS.

PS Helps Revitalize the Declining Brain

Dr. Crook eventually left the government research system and set up an international research group to conduct controlled human testing on possible therapies for AAMI, Alzheimer's, and other forms of cognitive decline. He worked with international teams drawn together from U.S. and overseas universities, hospitals and the private sector to evaluate a great number of pharmaceuticals and nutraceuticals. Then he got an opportunity to evaluate PS. It turned out to be, in his words, the single best agent for memory he had tested.

After producing very promising results in a number of successful clinical trials in Europe, PS came to the attention of Dr. Crook and his colleagues. Together with other highly competent colleagues in Italy, they conducted two double blind trials on PS. Both trials were well designed, passed scientific peer review and were published in respected U.S. journals. The first trial used PS against AAMI, the second against Alzheimer's dementia.

The double blind, randomized, placebo-controlled trial by Crook's team on AAMI (also called age-related cognitive decline at that time) used test protocols that were the state of the medical art.[17] In addition to Dr. Crook, backed by his regular MAC team, clinicians from Vanderbilt University School of Medicine in Nashville, Tennessee and the Stanford University School of Medicine in Palo Alto, California participated, as did prominent Italian researchers.

This was also a multicenter trial. The researchers recruited 149 subjects ages 50 to 75 years. The clinicians took the necessary careful steps to ensure these subjects fit the AAMI criteria to be included, and that subjects with symptoms of depression, stroke and other brain damage were excluded. The pool of subjects was then randomized into two groups; one group received PS at 300 mg per day, the other group received a placebo, for a total 12 weeks.

A sophisticated neuropsychological test battery was employed to measure various aspects of learning, attention, and memory. Subjects were assessed at baseline prior to the study's beginning, then three, six, nine and 12 weeks until dosing ceased, then once again at four weeks after the dosing was stopped.

After the dosing period ended and the blinded data was decoded, the PS group showed statistically significant improvement over the placebo on tests of memory and other cognitive abilities (for a simplified explanation of the meaning of the test statistics, see the box on page 18).

After the first three weeks of treatment, the PS group was scoring significantly better than the placebo group. Benefits of PS included better performance on memory tests such as name recall, telephone number recall, facial recognition, and object placement (keys and glasses). At the trial's end, after 12 weeks of treatment, the differences in favor of PS remained highly statistically significant ($p<0.01$ or lower). PS was calculated to improve memory performance as much as 30 percent over placebo.

Though clinically meaningful for the subjects in the PS group, this degree of benefit was not felt to be spectacular by Crook and his colleagues. But upon deeper inspection they found that a subgroup of the PS subjects had experienced markedly more benefit from PS. These turned out to be individuals who had the worst scores when the trial began.

This subgroup of worse-off subjects were slightly older at the trial's beginning, averaging 64.3 years versus 61.6 for the other subjects. With PS, they improved significantly better than placebo on a greater number of measures:

➡ Recognizing faces
➡ Learning names and faces
➡ Remembering names and faces
➡ Remembering telephone numbers
➡ Remembering a paragraph recently read
➡ Locating misplaced objects (keys, glasses, etc.)
➡ Concentrating while reading, conversing, performing tasks.

The data on Name-Face Acquisition (learning to match names together with faces) proved especially statistically reliable, so the researchers decided to use this as a model to calculate just how much PS had helped the more affected subgroup. They were able

What Statistical p Values Mean

Science merely represents humanity's best effort to systematize our subjective observations. Statistics help bring these subjective observations closer to being objective.

No observation can be guaranteed 100% correct with a zero chance of being wrong. Statistical methods were developed to generate probabilities of being correct. Thus in any controlled scientific experiment, including human clinical trials, the data collected are statistically processed and at the end emerge the p (probability) values.

Among life science researchers, usually the highest acceptable probability that an observation could be wrong is 5 percent. This calls for accepting a maximum $p<0.05$ ("p less than 0.05"), meaning less than 5% (5 chances in 100) that the observation is wrong and greater than 95% (95 chances in 100) that the observation is right. The $p<0.05$ value is often simply termed "statistically significant." A $p<0.01$ probability value would be nicer, since it means a 99% chance of being right and only a 1% chance of being wrong. This is usually termed "highly statistically significant." Then comes the $p<0.001$ value (99.9% versus 0.1%). Occasionally p values come out lower, and the lower they go, the greater the chance that the particular observation could be right.

to calculate that on this measure of mental function, PS had "rolled back the clock" by roughly 12 years.

In other words, from being at a functional, "cognitive age" equivalent to a typical person at age 64, the more afflicted subgroup was restored, on average, to a cognitive age of 52. Dr. Crook and his co-authors were very impressed by this degree of benefit, and stated at the end of their research publication, "The magnitude of effect from PS may be considered significant by many subjects and clinicians."[17]

The success of this double blind trial by Crook's group helped validate a more modest AAMI-type trial on PS, not double blind, and conducted in Italy in 1987 by Sinforiani and collaborators.[19] Crook and his collaborators' modernized testing, the precise and real-life nature of Crook's test methods, and the use of sophisticated software for the statistical analysis, altogether give strong support to their conclusion that PS can partially rejuvenate memory.

The Crook team's impressive findings with PS represent a nutrient that (unlike pharmaceuticals) is well tolerated by our living cells because it is orthomolecular.[20] Another feature of PS the orthomolecule is that it is fundamental to the brain's diverse functions. PS is essential to the cell membranes that run the brain cells that are organized into the nerve networks that make up the brain. That PS can be helpful to people badly afflicted with AAMI makes it possible that intervening with PS at the AAMI stage could help prevent dementia.

Next we look at the efforts by Dr. Crook's team and others to employ PS against Alzheimer's and other dementia.

CHAPTER 3

Useful Tool Against Severe Memory Loss

- Severe impairment of memory and other brain functions (dementia) is now epidemic in industrialized societies.
- PS sometimes will benefit brain function and sociability in persons with severe memory impairment.
- Practicing Total Health Management creates possibilities for further benefit from taking PS.

Severe memory impairment in the form of dementia is now epidemic in the industrialized countries. For the United States, as one example, reliable statistics from the Alzheimer's Association of the United States indicate that more than 7.5 million citizens have some form of dementia.[21] The Association has estimated that for Americans aged 65 and over the risk of developing Alzheimer's dementia is about 1 in 10. For those past age 85, the risk is as high as 1 in 2! Not good odds for any of us.

Dementia doesn't come out of nowhere. Dementia is the end result of years, probably decades, of progressive deterioration of the brain tissue. As it inevitably comes to afflict the entire brain beyond just the memory centers, dementia represents an extreme state of brain deterioration that is very difficult to treat by any means.

Abnormal Memory Decline Can Lead to Dementia

Dementia emerges from the progressive worsening of memory impairment. As introduced in the previous chapter, the conditions AAMI, ARCD, and MCI all feature measurable memory loss that is abnormal for that sample population. None of these is currently classified as a disease, but having any of them means having a higher risk for dementia than others in one's age group. Having this degree of memory problem is a wake-up call to immediately take positive steps.

There is much about dementia that science and medicine do not understand, but one fact is clear: Memory loss is usually progressive. Memory loss gets worse unless positive steps are taken to revitalize the brain. As the extent of memory impairment becomes ever more severe, there is less and less healthy tissue to work with, so that the chances of turning it around become ever more slim. At some point the degree of memory and other cognitive impairment will cross the line into dementia.

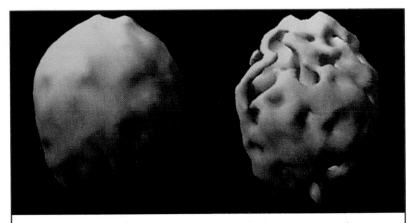

SPECT scanning shows empty spaces in the brain matrix where function is below normal. *Left*, healthy brain, imaged top-down, front of brain facing down. *Right*, Alzheimer's Disease brain, in same orientation. Note the large network of empty zones, all showing abnormally poor function. From Amen.[22]

The formal diagnosis of dementia can be made when the subject has severe memory impairment as well as impairment of one or more of the other measurable cognitive functions. Stedman's *Pocket Medical Dictionary* defines cognition as: "the quality of knowing, which includes perceiving, recognizing, conceiving, judging, sensing, reasoning, and imagining." These are the mental capacities that most make us human. Dementia is diagnosed when these capacities are grossly affected.

Dementia as Daily Existence
The term dementia is related to "de-mens" (out of mind) or "de-mentation," translating as loss of mental capacity, loss of the capacity to reason. The disease of dementia marks a degree of cognitive deterioration so severe that social and occupational functioning is markedly impaired. Imagine the devastating consequences of not being able to think for yourself or otherwise take care of your basic survival needs.

The costs of dementia to the family and society are also great.

The Alzheimer's Association in the U.S. estimates that Alzheimer's care costs American families close to $19,000 a year and that the total cost to the nation in health care and lost productivity could be more than $100 billion. Also, more than 70 percent of Alzheimer's patients are cared for at home, and the victim's tragic situation often comes to include the persons who have to care for them.

The progression of dementia mercilessly destroys its victim's humanity. Along with the relentless deterioration of cognitive capacities can come radical change in the personality, as other zones of the brain deteriorate. That previously mild-mannered, friendly, thoughtful relative can become aggressive, irascible, vulgar, the very opposite of what s/he was like as a younger person.

As the dementia progresses, that person may no longer be able to recall the things we all automatically file in our consciousness: what clothes they wore yesterday or the day before, where they went, what they ate, who they last talked with. They may no longer recognize close relatives. As their waning attentiveness signals to them that something is very wrong, they can withdraw from social life.

The patient with worsening dementia may reach a point where s/he has to be assisted with the most basic life functions like eating, washing, going to the bathroom—known medically as the "Activities of Daily Living." The average Alzheimer's patient lives some 8–20 years after being diagnosed.

Currently, the majority of diagnosed dementias are thought to be Alzheimer's Disease, but the Alzheimer's symptoms are often mimicked by other forms of dementia. On a symptomatic basis there is little to distinguish between them. The medical management strategy doesn't differ very much, either. Modern medicine, with all its technology, still has very little to offer this patient population.

There is no cure for Alzheimer's or the other dementias, and no breakthrough on the horizon. Currently there are three drugs currently approved to treat dementia. All are only minimally beneficial and many experts have noticed that their benefits tend to disappear after a year or two. Also, these drugs carry significant risk of bad side effects. Pharmaceuticals are no antidote for dementia.

All this makes clear that the best strategy against dementia is to prevent it from developing at all. But for those who already have dementia and for their loved ones, this option no longer exists. Their daunting challenge is to preserve as much as possible of the brain, for as long as possible. This is where PS offers some chance for improvement, but only as part of a total health management program.

Total Health Management (THM) for a long and happy life

THM means living actively by:

★ Exercising body, mind, and spirit
★ Avoiding chemical and physical toxic stressors, as well as emotional stress
★ Using nutrients to optimize the life functions, especially those orthomolecules proven very safe to use
★ Working with an integrative healthy practitioner trained to assess total health
★ Making the necessary lifestyle changes to support these activities
★ Turning to pharmaceuticals and other potentially life-threatening interventions only as a last resort.

In this toxic modern world, daily practice of THM is our best chance to experience our birthright of excellent health. Practicing THM gives us—whatever our age or stage of life—a real chance to cure, slow, or reverse biological dysfunctions that are obstacles to our happiness.

Total Health Management Can Delay Dementia

To conserve brain and mind and all the other features of good health, our best (and only) chance for a long and healthy life is to learn and practice total health management (THM). THM works best as a daily style of living, a manner of living that self-consciously takes into account all the factors that can positively or negatively impact our health. THM really is lifestyle, consciously integrating all the activities of daily life into a harmonious whole, untiringly urging the body and spirit toward health and happiness.

For those who have dementia or are progressing toward dementia, the daily practice of THM can help not only the patient but the caregiver and all others to avoid a similar fate. Intervening with THM at this relatively late stage amounts to a kind of brain circuit conservation. Using PS (and other safe brain nutrients) as part of the THM strategy additionally allows for the possibility of reactivating sick circuits, promoting the brain's marvelous circuit adaptability (called "plasticity"), and possibly even to create new circuitry.

Current brain research is at a fascinating point: it's clear that the brain is extremely plastic, surprisingly capable of remolding existing circuits to replace lost ones. Also, the brain has powerful cells called stem cells, unspecialized reserve cells able to specialize into new nerve cells when called for. For these regenerative processes to be set in motion, it's likely that (a) degenerative processes already in place must be curbed; (b) sufficient mental activity must be occurring to stimulate regeneration (the brain must be used); (c) nutrients must be supplied that support the formation of new cells and circuits. All this is possible once the practice of THM is adopted and set into motion.

The first THM issue for successful, ongoing brain conservation is risk factor recognition and prevention. A number of factors are known to raise or lower the risk for dementia. So many of these are known that I speak of a dementia risk factor matrix (see page 26). By eliminating or lessening the negative factors, and reinforcing the positive factors, the THM person can substantially conserve his brain and in many instances experience a degree of cognitive rejuvenation.

The Matrix of Risk Factors for Dementia

As with other diseases, dementia is associated with risk factors of various sorts.[23] Any of us can reduce or eliminate at least some of our risk factors, once we know what they are. The dementia risk factors differ in their degrees of impact on each individual, but all are known to initiate brain problems or make existing problems worse.

On a practical basis it's good to think of the dementia risk factors as making up a matrix. This matrix is a multi-dimensional interaction of the various risk factors as they vary in time of onset, duration, severity, and the relative degrees of interaction with each other. By implication, a risk factor matrix will be unique to each individual, and that person's gene makeup will have unique interactions with the matrix, actually being part of the matrix itself.

Let's look at a conservative assessment of risk factors for dementia, that is, staying with those factors most proven by science. This makes for a likely understated estimate of the risk factors. Even on an understated basis the matrix is considerable.[23-25]

➡ **PRIOR BRAIN INJURY** is probably the single best proven risk factor for dementia. One or more of these can initiate the

---

Dementia Risk Factor Matrix[23]

Very Likely Risk Factors: Prior brain injury; homozygosity (two doses) of apolipoprotein E-4; advanced age; family history of dementia or Parkinson's disease; Down Syndrome; alcohol abuse; depression, stroke, reduced blood flow to the brain.

Likely Risk Factors: Long-term coronary heart disease, emotional stress, smoking; pollutant solvents, herbicides, pesticides; certain pharmaceuticals; nutrient deficiencies, metabolic deficits; hypertension; underactivity (mental or physical); low educational level.

---

dementia pugilistica of brain-damaged boxers, which clinically is hardly different from any other dementia. Just one concussion injury to the brain can increase the risk for dementia in later life to about four times (4x the usual risk).

➡ **BAD GENES** can act as dementia risk factors. The most well known is ApoE4 (apolipoprotein E4). Homozygosity for ApoE4 (that is, two doses of this gene) increase the risk of Alzheimer's.[26] Yet ApoE4's penetrance (fancy term for the gene's degree of control over the outcome) is far from complete. That is, many of the people homozygous for ApoE4 will have a normal lifespan without developing Alzheimer's.

Both the above risk factors contribute to risk factor synergy. This is the unfortunate reality, that having one risk factor can multiply the danger from another risk factor. For example, a person who sustained a head trauma might have about a 4-time risk of getting dementia. Another who is homozygous for ApoE4 also might have about a 4-time risk. But a person with previous brain trauma AND homozygous for ApoE4 has about a 10-fold risk of getting Alzheimer's.[23]

➡ **FOR ALL DEMENTIA, OTHER HIGHLY PROBABLE RISK FACTORS** are Down syndrome (DS), depression, poor circulation to the brain (as with ex-smokers and/or drinkers). Down Syndrome has a major genetic component, yet many DS people are quite intelligent and many do not get dementia.

➡ **HYPERTENSION, STROKE, AND DIABETES ARE MAJOR FACTORS FOR VASCULAR DEMENTIA.** Poor brain circulation is more linked to vascular dementia (VD) than to Alzheimer's, but clinically VD can be just as devastating. VD or its earliest manifestation can sometimes be helped by total health management. THM for VD especially should emphasize regular aerobic exercise to increase blood supply to the brain.

➡ **ENVIRONMENTAL POLLUTANTS DAMAGE THE BRAIN.** Brain tissue is vulnerable to toxins of any kind, because it has an high metabolic rate and also because of its very high content of polyunsaturated fats. Toxins are brain stressors. The massive degree to which mercury and other heavy metals, solvents, and pesticides and herbicides now contaminate the planetary environment makes it virtually certain they are contributing to today's escalating incidence of dementia.[27]

➡ **MANY PHARMACEUTICALS ARE BRAIN TOXINS**, legally sanctioned and even promoted for consumption by the general population. The toxicity of some can mimic dementia over the short term. As much as 10 percent of all apparent dementia cases may be induced by sleep aids, sedatives, antidepressants, or drugs from other categories.[28] Fortunately these are reversible to some degree, if the responsible physician is sufficiently alert to make the connection. One exceptionally useful reference book for this purpose is *Worst Pills, Best Pills*, collectively authored by the Public Citizen Health Research Group of Washington, D.C.

➡ **EMOTIONAL STRESS KILLS BRAIN CELLS.** A long-term clinical study done at McGill University in Canada[29] tracked two groups of people for five years. These were good stress copers and bad stress copers. After five years, the bad stress copers had statistically greater damage to the brain's main memory-creating zone, the hippocampus. Other human studies and many animal studies altogether prove that mental stress can kill nerve cells in the hippocampus and effectively disable this memory zone of the brain. [29, 30]

The ongoing outcome of negative risk factors is to deplete circuits from the brain. At its peak performance state, which usually is reached in the early twenties, the human brain can have upwards of 10,000 connections for each of its approximately 100 billion nerve cells. This yields a "ball-park" figure of as many as 1,000 trillion cell-to-cell connections—a quadrillion separate pathways. But as it progresses toward dementia, the brain is suffering awesome circuit losses.

Consider the brain's cortex, for example. Elderly people in their eighties who are not demented, may have lost up to 20 percent of

PS (PhosphatidylSerine)

their connections. In contrast, Alzheimer's patients upon autopsy can have lost up to 90 percent.[31]

Unbelievably, this may not be the worst. For the hippocampus, the brain region that normally initiates new memories, the damage from dementia may be more extreme. An Alzheimer's patient may lose just about all of the hippocampal CA1 cells crucial for memory formation.[31]

No one can expect to escape this tragic personal fate unless first they have eliminated the many known negative risk factors for dementia from their life. Secondly, they have to practice total health management with commitment and discipline. An important part of THM for the brain is to take advantage of nutrients that are safe over the long term, have proven brain benefits, and have shown real benefits in dementia. On the short list that exists, PS is at the top.

PS Double Blind Trials Show Benefit Against Dementia
A number of double blind trials have been conducted with PS on Alzheimer's and non-Alzheimer's dementia. The first double blind trial with PS on Alzheimer's was conducted in Belgium by Delwaide and colleagues, and published in 1986.[32] A summary of this trial is provided in Appendix 1.

The Delwaide trial found that PS significantly improved many of the "activities of daily living" for these dementia patients. These included personal grooming, dressing, feeding, bowel control, bladder control, ability to go to the toilet unaided, and verbal expression. After only six weeks, PS at 300 mg per day had made a real difference to Alzheimer's patients and their families. The authors noted, "…the changes observed in the present study reflect an improvement in behavior which can be useful for patients and their families."

The next double blind Alzheimer's trial with PS was the Italian Multicenter Study of Dementia, carried out by 22 researchers working in seven Italian neurology research centers. Coordinated by Professor Luigi Amaducci, its findings were published in 1988.[33] Perhaps because a lower dose of PS was used in this trial (200 mg per day), it took six months for the full effect of PS to come through. There was a statistical trend toward benefit from PS that fell short of the minimum required 95 percent probability. Within the PS group, however, a subgroup of the most severely afflicted patients had derived statistically significant benefit from PS as compared to placebo. An interesting outcome of this trial is

28

that these severe patients continued to improve for three months following the end of dosing with PS.

Then came the 1992 double blind trial by Dr. Tom Crook and his international collaborators.[18] Using their advanced testing methodology, along with global clinical assessments done both by physicians and by the patients' family members, they also found that PS was useful for Alzheimer's. It could not be called a breakthrough therapy, but after three weeks on the 300 mg daily dose of PS, and continuing through the three months of the trial, the PS group performed significantly better on tests such as memory for names of familiar persons, misplaced object recall, details of events from the previous day, and details of events from within the past week.

In this trial, a subgroup of patients who were the least afflicted when they entered the trial were found to derive the most benefit from PS. These mild Alzheimer's patients significantly improved their ability to concentrate while on PS, became less inclined to complain that their memory was deteriorating, and showed significant improvement over placebo when assessed by physicians. Dr. Crook's group concluded that PS offered meaningful, if modest, benefit to patients with mild Alzheimer's progression.

Later came a large Italian multicenter double blind trial, coordinated by Cenacchi and published in 1993.[34] This trial established that PS could be administered long-term (up to six months) to elderly patients taking a variety of drugs, without increasing the risk of bad side effects. The group who received PS at 300 mg per day had significantly improved memory and learning on a word test, also improved motivation and overall awareness. Crook and colleagues concluded, "The resulting improvements in adaptability to the environment can have an important impact on the quality of life of such patients."

Other trials were conducted with PS on dementia patients, with varying designs and looking at a variety of clinical and physiological measures. Taking all these trials into consideration, it is clear that PS is not a single-nutrient therapy for dementia, but it does offer some degree of value.

For some of these patients with dementia, PS achieved limited improvement of cognitive functions. For the majority of these patients, PS improved Activities of Daily Living, including personal hygiene and the other daily personal tasks that healthy people take

PS (PhosphatidylSerine)

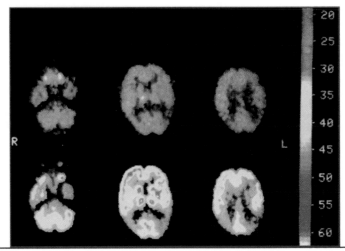

PET scanning measures energy production in the brain. This woman with Alzheimer's had very poor energy production (top row of scans) until after receiving PS at 500 mg per day for three weeks (bottom row). Note the scale at right, with yellow and red being the highest energy levels. From Klinkhammer and colleagues.[7]

for granted. In these respects PS seems to be as good as, or better than, any other single intervention for dementia.

Even for patients with full-blown Alzheimer's, PS sometimes would make a measurable difference to brain function. One German study with PS used high-technology "PET" imaging (positron emission tomography) to measure energy production across the brain in patients with advanced Alzheimer's. They displayed significantly enhanced brain activity after taking PS for three weeks at up to 500 mg per day.

However much PS does benefit a patient with dementia, the considerable clinical evidence available to us makes one thing clear: the earlier people start on PS, the better the result they can hope to get. The chances to slow or possibly partially reverse the declining cognitive functions are much better if the individual is started on PS at the stage of AAMI or some other stage less advanced than the dementia diagnosis.

The chapters that follow move beyond using PS for memory and cognition into detailing its proven usefulness also to improve mood, anxiety, and coping with mental or physical stress. As these themes are developed, the superiority of PS, the orthomolecular nutrient, continues to be evident, so also does the relevance of total health management to fuller realization of the benefits of PS.

CHAPTER 4

Lifting Depression and Anxiety

- Clinical depression and the associated anxiety is more prevalent even than dementia and carries a high risk of suicide.
- Clinical trials indicate PS can improve mood and relieve anxiety.
- Experimental studies suggest PS is working at the cell membrane level, via a fundamental signaling mechanism that facilitates potent clinical action.

Clinical depression, most often termed major depressive disorder, is more than four times as prevalent as dementia. Latest estimates place the number of clinically depressed people in the USA at minimally 40 million. This number does not include patients with the related bipolar disorder or manic-depression, who probably number another 5–10 million. Depression carries with it the burdens of despair and often also, an increased contemplation of ending one's life.

Typically, depression is associated with changes in appetite and sleep patterns, fatigue, difficulty with concentration, poor self-image, and feelings of hopelessness, to the extent that productivity and social functioning are impaired. And all too often, depression is accompanied by cognitive impairment of a degree that can mimic dementia.

The drugs used for depression, while being heavily promoted, can have major and sometimes life-threatening side effects. Any intervention that is safe to use over the long-term is worthy of investigation.

Trials With PS for Depression and Anxiety

PS has been put through a number of double blind and other controlled human studies to combat depression and anxiety. Taken together, the findings from these studies prove it can benefit mood and help lift depression.

As early as 1981, Sengupta and fellow researchers[35] reported that patients with clinical depression had abnormally low amounts of PS in cells of their blood (platelets and red cells). This study suggested that clinical depression could be linked to PS deficiency.

In 1990, Rabboni and colleagues published a trial on PS for depression in elderly patients.[36] This was an open trial, in which both the researchers and the patients knew that all the patients were receiving PS. There were three groups, each of 10 patients, (1) those with Alzheimer's dementia, (2) those with non-Alzheimer's dementia, and (3) those not demented, but clinically depressed. All three groups received PS at 400 mg per day for 60 days.

By 30 days into the trial, PS had significantly improved all three groups, and the statistical p score for the group with depression was the best (p<0.01, meaning less than one chance in 100 that the finding was due to chance). The improvements from PS were still in place at day 60, and continued to day 90 for all three groups, notably a full 30 days after the PS dosing was discontinued. Even for an open trial, which is less reliable than a double blind trial, these benefits from PS are impressive.

Then a double blind trial found that PS could relieve depression and anxiety, along with improving memory and other cognitive functions. Maggioni and colleagues[39] recruited for this trial 10 women ages 70 to 81 (average 73.3 years). All were hospitalized with major depression. Having this diagnosis means they reported being in a depressed mood on the majority of days over a period of two years or more. Along with their depression these elderly women also had abnormal anxiety and their cognitive functions were so bad they mimicked dementia. They were first given a placebo for 15 days to "wash out" previous treatments, then put on 300 mg PS per day for 45 days.

When evaluated on the 45th day, the patients showed dramatic improvement in their depression, as scored by the well validated Hamilton Rating Scale. The statistical significance of the finding was very high (p<0.001, meaning less than one chance in 1,000 that the finding was due to chance). Several other well-accepted rating scales were used to assess their mental state. Their anxiety also scored dramatically improved, again at p<0.001. PS also significantly benefited their memory, attention and concentration. Their irritability improved, along with a wide range of other emotional functions. Their "sociability" also markedly improved.

PS clearly benefited depression and anxiety in women. But does it do the same for men? In a 1995 double blind trial, Gindin and collaborators used subjects of both genders.[37] They recruited 57 patients ages 60–80, all with memory problems that fell short of dementia, and none clinically depressed when the trial began. They were randomly assigned to two groups, one to receive placebo and the other 300 mg PS a day for three months. The trial occurred during a time of the year that the "winter blues" can arise. The placebo group developed some depressive symptoms reminiscent of the winter blues, while the PS group did not. Both the men and the women seemed to do better on PS.

An earlier trial by Manfredi and colleagues[38] investigated PS for mood, but it was administered each day by injection rather than by mouth. However the results obtained were consistent with the results obtained using PS as a dietary supplement. This 1987 trial recruited 40 elderly women who had poor blood supply to the brain and suffered "psychosomatic disturbances inherent to menopause and senility."[38] All were already receiving a "basic therapy" that consisted of vasodilator drugs, flunarizine, and citicoline. They were divided into two groups; one group received 50 mg PS by intramuscular injection each day, the other received no PS.

After 30 days the PS group scored significant improvements in their anxiety, insomnia, memory, and overall weakness and debility over the group that did not get PS. Depression was reported markedly reduced in 80 percent of those in the PS group, compared to 50 percent of those who did not get PS. Worthy of note is that adding in PS gave additional benefits beyond those of the basic therapy, which included the phospholipid precursor citicoline. This nutrient is consistently less effective than PS, probably because it requires a lot of energy to be converted into membrane phospholipids.

PS Mood Benefits Are Likely Based in Membranes
In the 1990 double blind trial by Maggioni and collaborators,[39] the researchers drew blood plasma samples from their elderly women subjects and looked for changes in chemical transmitter status. They found no alterations in the levels of the major transmitters serotonin, norepinephrine, dopamine, all of which are linked to depression and other mood alterations. This lack of effect on transmitter levels suggested PS may be having more subtle effects in the brain, probably through effects at the cell membrane level.

In 1996 Maggioni and his colleagues reported on another controlled trial in which they gave PS to depressed elderly women (average age 72 years) and took blood samples to assess their endorphin status.[40] The hypothesis was that PS might elevate mood through elevating endorphins. Ten women with depression (eight with major depression and two bipolar or manic-depressive), were matched with 10 healthy controls and 10 young controls (average age 29 years). All received PS at 200 mg per day for 30 days.

At the study's end, the depression group had significantly improved on the Hamilton Scale, a scale commonly used to quantify degree of depression. However, their blood mononuclear cells did not show higher endorphins in comparison to the two control groups. Again, this study's outcome points away from individual transmitter changes and toward a more profound effect from PS consistent with its membrane action.

Advances in the science of depression and other mood disorders suggest that one major underlying abnormality is in signal transduction. This is an array of processes occurring at the level of the cell membrane, whereby signals reaching the cell from the outside are converted by the membrane into signals that reach the cell interior.[41] PS is a key phospholipid for membrane function and is known to be centrally involved in signal transduction in brain cells.

There is also highly suggestive evidence from clinical trials that long chain omega-3 fatty acids (DHA at least, probably EPA as well) are centrally involved in mood control at the level of cell membrane signal transduction. Especially considering that PS and DHA have a kind of mother-daughter relationship in brain cell membranes, these two nutrient sets are likely to have synergistic benefit for mood and anxiety when taken together. This topic is discussed in the upcoming chapter on PS and DHA.

People don't have to be old or clinically depressed to get into a better mood from taking PS. The benefits of this remarkable brain nutrient for mood and anxiety in younger people are discussed in the next chapter.

CHAPTER 5

Disarming Mental Stress, A Memory Killer

- Emotional stress, when sustained for long periods, will kill brain cells and increase the risk for dementia. The mechanisms are well-known.
- Taking PS made it easier for young volunteers to handle the stress of doing mental arithmetic without a calculator.
- PS can partially rejuvenate the stress coping mechanisms in older people.
- By taking PS and practicing total health management, it is possible to lessen the ravages of stress on the brain and likely lower the risk of dementia.

Mental ("emotional") stress could be the most underrated cause of suffering, lost productivity, and premature death in modern society. Also, solid research has shown it is an awesome destroyer of memory. Stress sustained over a long period causes chronic, abnormal elevation of circulating stress hormones that can kill off brain cells. From this negative effect of emotional stress can come increased risk for dementia.

All living things practice *homeostasis*—the ability to maintain the constancy of their internal environment. Homeostasis is essential to maintain life, and our brain tissue must maintain homeostasis along with all our other tissues. For our enzymes and other catalytic biomolecules to work at their best, the physical and chemical conditions must be held very close to constant.

Any agent or factor that threatens to disrupt homeostasis is called a stressor. Too much of almost anything can become a stressor. According to the now-classic understanding of stress pioneered by Professor Hans Selye,[42] a manageable amount of challenge to homeostasis is good "practice" for stress management—this he called *eustress*. But stressors that are too powerful can push the system far out of balance and threaten to exceed the body's capacity to return to homeostasis. Stress to this extreme degree *(distress)* can trigger disease or even cause death. Common human stressors include heat, cold, dehydration, starvation, lack of sleep, toxic exposures, infections, radiation, vibration, noise, and emotional challenges of whatever sort.

Along with other higher animals, we humans have what is called The Stress Response. It helps us survive any of these stressors (or combinations of them) that seem to pose an immediate challenge to survival. It was probably very important in keeping our species around for this long. It involves a cascade of physiological adjustments that occur rapidly and on demand. This cascade is normally mediated mainly by the hormone cortisol.

The classic Stress Response develops as the brain's hypothalamus region perceives the threat, then stimulates the pituitary master gland to secrete ACTH (AdrenoCorticoTropic Hormone), which hormone in turn pushes the adrenals to secrete cortisol into the blood. These glands, acting in coordination, are called the Hypothalamic Pituitary Adrenal Axis, or HPAA for short.

The HPAA helps the body successfully handle a stressful incident or situation, but it was designed to be sustained only for a short time, on the order of minutes or hours or possibly days, not for weeks and months or years. Faced with sustained emotional stress, the human body will successfully adapt at first, but as time goes by, this adaptation can run out of energy. As a consequence, long-term stress of any kind is bad for our bodies, but high cortisol over a long period can have an especially bad impact on our brain cells.

Fight or Flight: Good Thing That Can Go Bad
The human Stress Response is a version of the animal Fight-or-Flight Response, a fundamental biological response to a stressful situation. It has the needed effect of activating and coordinating the body's organ systems to cope with a short-term emergency, then to return to the normal way of living as quickly as possible. But in today's chaotic world, the emergencies that confront us are too often long-term rather than immediate. This makes for a problem—when fight or flight has to be sustained, it can deplete the body's resources and move it in a frighteningly negative direction.

The human brain is a gas-guzzling organ. With only 3 percent of the body's mass, the brain at rest consumes more than 20 percent of the body's energy. With intense mental activity the brain can be using as much as 60 percent of the body's energy. The nerve cells are the body's largest cells—motor nerve cells can reach four feet long, for example. They are also our busiest cells—their constant electrical activity demands a lot of energy. This is what makes them so vulnerable to poor circulation or lack of oxygen. High cortisol in the brain from stress has this very effect.

Why Don't Zebras Get Ulcers? Or Dementia?

Stanford professor Robert Sapolsky has spent much of his career studying animals under stress in the wild. His book *Why Zebras Don't Get Ulcers* [30] brilliantly answers its own question.

When the zebra senses a predator, its stress response goes into action. Adrenaline and noradrenaline surge into the bloodstream. Glucose comes surging out of storage tissues into the blood, to provide instant energy. The heart beats faster, the breathing rate increases, to get more oxygen and nutrients to the tissues. Stress hormones divert blood flow away from the brain and into the muscles, to help flee the imminent danger.

For this few minutes that it takes to escape the oncoming lion, the zebra's physiology is controlled by the stress response. Its higher brain functions give way to naked instinctual behavior in order to escape this danger. Then things calm down; having outrun the lion, after just a few minutes the zebra can return to meditating as it grazes.

For humans, the situation is different. The zebra only has stress as a short-term, occasional event, while we modern humans face continual, unrelenting stress. Most of us live in a state of stress almost all the time. Unfortunately, our biological means for coping with stress have remained basically the same as the zebra's. Prof. Sapolsky asks wryly, "How many hippos worry about whether Social Security is going to last, or even what they are going to say on a first date."

The work of Sapolsky, along with that of Lupien on humans,[29] and many other researchers, joins with Selye's to send a clear message: for humans under sustained stress, the physiological fight-or-flight response becomes pathologic. It drives the individual into disease. We become mental casualties of chronic stress.

As the body prepares for fight-or-flight, cortisol is released into the circulating blood. Cortisol increases blood flow to the muscles (to fight or flee!), and to come up with this extra blood it reduces the blood going to the brain. However, the brain has such a high demand for blood circulation to supply the nerve cells that maintaining fight-or-flight beyond a mere few minutes can threaten the brain's ability to continue to function.

The nerve cells of the hippocampus and cortex brain regions are our best and brightest cells—they initiate and consolidate experiences into memory. But they are extra vulnerable to high cortisol. Continued high levels of circulating cortisol have been shown to cause the hippocampus to shrink ("atrophy"). As this brain region loses functional circuits, so also does its owner lose the capacity to make new memories.

Emotional stress can act synergistically on the hippocampus with other stressors. The nerve cells are highly vulnerable to "free radicals" and other toxins because they carry high amounts of fats in their outer insulation (myelin). These fats are easily destroyed by mercury, lead, or other heavy metals, by solvents and other organic environmental pollutants, and by any number of other toxic substances.

The brain is equipped with antioxidant defenses to help protect against such stressors, but these can be compromised by poor eating habits, lack of exercise and poor circulation, blood sugar fluctuations, over-consumption of prescription drugs, and many other deleterious factors. All these factors are stressors that compound the damage from emotional stress.

A number of controlled trials and other human studies have been done with PS for stress. Their findings suggest that taking PS can make a real difference in our capacity to manage a stressful challenge while keeping our stress hormones from getting out of control.

PS Helps Students Manage Mental Stress

Dr. David Benton of the University of Wales is a famous researcher on nutrition and mental performance, and has published many groundbreaking studies on children and other youth. In 2001, together with colleagues, he published a double blind trial that indicated PS improved mental performance in some of his male students whom he experimentally subjected to stress.[43]

Forty-eight male university students, average age 20.8 years, were randomly divided into a PS test group (300 mg/day) and a placebo group. Each student's "baseline" mood—how he felt over the previous week—was assessed by questionnaire, and a mood score developed from it. They also were scored for "neuroticism" and "extroversion." Blood pressure, pulse, and heart rate were recorded, then each subject was sent home with a 30-day supply of PS or placebo at three capsules per day.

After 30 days of supplementation the subjects returned to the laboratory. They reported their mood over the last week of supplementation. They then faced a standard acute stress test: a challenging mental arithmetic calculation to be done within four seconds, and without a calculator! Their heart rates increased during the test and this combined with the students' self-reports to confirm that they did find the test stressful. After the test was completed, their blood pressure was recorded and their mood assessed again.

The results showed that those students with a more "neurotic" personality experienced significantly less stress from the test, if they were on PS. Those who had been receiving only placebo reported a highly significant level of stress from the test and experienced a highly significant worsening of mood ($p<0.001$). Their counterparts who got PS did not deteriorate in mood.

Individuals who score high on tests for neuroticism are known to respond more poorly to stress, and typically report more distress in daily life. In this trial, the "neurotics" who took PS were not significantly stressed by the test. Their mood remained stable; they scored significantly better on feeling clear-headed, composed, and confident. Through taking PS they were better able to deal with the time-limited challenge of doing mental arithmetic the old-fashioned way.

PS Revitalizes the Stress Response in the Elderly

Other clinical research indicates PS may help revitalize fading HPAA function in the elderly, to help them cope with their perceived mental stress.

The Dexamethasone Suppression Test can be used to test how well the stress response works in an aging person. In young, healthy people 1 mg of dexamethasone (a synthetic glucocorticoid that resembles cortisol) suppresses the production of cortisol and other adrenal steroid hormones linked to the stress response. This suppression usually lasts for more than 24 hours. But many older people do not show this suppression by DEX. Called Early Cortisol Escape, this phenomenon is thought to indicate deterioration of the HPA axis in the elderly.

Dr. Dina Nerozzi and co-researchers at the University of Rome found that by giving PS supplements (at 300 mg per day) to elderly men and women for 60 days, they could restore the youthful capacity for DEX suppression.[44] They suggested that PS was restoring faded pituitary function, either by stimulating nerve cells to organize into new networks and/or by returning brain chemical transmitter levels toward a more youthful balance.

In their study with depressed elderly patients, Rabboni's group in Milan had some patients who showed poor DEX suppression at the start.[36] After being on PS at 400 mg per day for 60 days, all nine of these patients had their capacity for DEX suppression restored. These researchers were so impressed with PS that they commented, "Phosphatidylserine could open the way to a new therapeutic conception: the possibility of influencing the complex inter-relations between the neurological, immunological and endocrine systems."[36]

PS Partially Rejuvenates Aging Brain Rhythms

In addition to revitalizing the aging hypothalamic-pituitary-adrenal axis, PS helps "tune up" the body's 24-hour daily "circadian" rhythms. As we age, these rhythms tend to become less synchronous, resulting in sleep problems and sometimes also hormonal imbalances. This loss of rhythm seems linked to pituitary gland decline, and probably also to decline of the brain's hypothalamus that supervises the pituitary.

Normally the "master" pituitary gland secretes a variety of hormones that coordinate these cycles by stimulating other glands to release other hormones. One important pituitary product is TSH, Thyroid Stimulating Hormone. TSH stimulates the thyroid gland to release thyroxin, which boosts metabolism. Masturzo and collaborators did a randomized, placebo-controlled trial on institutionalized elderly men with abnormally low TSH hormone secretion. [45]

Going into the trial, these 20 elderly male patients (ages 65 to 85, average age 73.7) were secreting TSH but at lower than youthful levels, and they did not have the youthful circadian rhythm.[45] The older they were, the more random was their pattern of TSH release. Ten (10) of these older men received PS (at 400 mg per day) for 30 days and 10 received a placebo. Another six men, ages 21–31 (average age 22.3 years), served as youthful controls and received no treatment. After 30 days, the elderly men who received PS showed a circadian rhythm of TSH secretion. Their circadian rhythm was comparable with the young male adult controls (mean age 22.3 years). Those elderly men who received only placebo showed no improvement of their random secretion.

Masturzo and her colleagues suggested that PS was working at the level of cell membranes to cause this rather remarkable benefit. As we recognize the benefits of PS for mental stress, we can recall that being an orthomolecule, PS naturally has a pro-homeostatic, anti-stress influence. Consider that PS works from the cell membrane level throughout the entire cell. Because it is naturally present in all our cells, its beneficial actions on single cells are amplified to benefit the body as a whole.

So PS can be working simultaneously in the hypothalamus, the pituitary, the adrenals, and elsewhere in the organs to keep our life processes within normal limits. Dietary supplementation with PS can help correct functions that are too low and lower them when they are too high. By these means PS can boost a weakened stress response in the elderly person and calm the tendency to exaggerated stress response in the young person.

CHAPTER 6

PS Also Helps
Manage Physical Stress

- Physical stress raises stress hormones just as mental (emotional) stress can do.
- PS lowers cortisol levels in young volunteers subjected to strenuous physical exercise.
- Taking PS also helped athletes avoid overtraining, a common experience of intense physical exercise.

Mental stress has its counterpart in physical stress. Excessive heat and cold, excessive noise, high radiation, high vibration, intense exercise, all are physical stressors. To cope with physical stress, the same HPAA mechanisms must kick in, operating much as they do for mental stress. Therefore, as with mental stressors, in response to physical stressors, cortisol and other stress hormones such as ACTH go up in the blood. If the brain's HPAA axis becomes excessively activated, the Stress Response again can threaten disease or even death. Similar to its proven benefits against mental stress, PS has shown usefulness against excessive physical stress.

PS Improves Physical Stress Management in Students

Dr. Benton's team did another double blind trial with PS on his young students. This time a physical stressor was used— intense exercise.[46] It is well-known that heart rate increases during demanding physical exercise. It can go up quite a lot, but the healthiest response to exercise is that the heart rate returns to normal as soon as possible after the exercise ends. This is especially important for people who take part in sports that require sprints or bouts of intense exercise. This second Benton trial investigated PS for heart rate control under just such conditions.[46]

Seventeen male university students were randomly divided into a PS group and a group that received placebo. Initial heart rate and blood pressure were measured and the subjects reported on their mood over the previous month. They then started on their prescribed intakes of PS (300 mg per day) or placebo and after 30 days returned to the laboratory.

In the laboratory each subject was fitted with a heart rate monitor, then vigorously pedaled an ergonomic bicycle for 20 minutes and rested for 40 minutes. It was found that during the second 10-minute exercise period, the PS subjects' heart rates did not increase as much as did those on placebo. It seems PS helped increase the heart's efficiency, so that heart rate did not spike in the face of the vigorous physical challenge. Benton suggested PS could be having this effect through optimizing the transport proteins for calcium and magnesium in the heart fiber membranes.

After the rest period the PS subjects were significantly more confident and composed, and in a better mood, as compared to the group that received placebo. This second double blind finding that PS improves coping with physical stress matches up with the earlier Benton finding that PS works against mental stress.

Improves Stress Hormone Status
Intense physical exercise can elevate circulating stress hormones. In 1992, Monteleone's group in Italy reported on a double blind, placebo-controlled trial that evaluated PS for stress hormone control in young, healthy men subjected to exercise-induced stress. This came from riding a stationary bicycle at a high speed until nearly exhausted.[47]

The riders took either PS (at 400 or 800 mg per day) or placebo, for 10 days. Then they reported to the exercise laboratory where their veins were cannulated to allow blood samples to be taken as necessary. Then they were made to pedal vigorously on a bicycle ergometer for 20 minutes. Their lactate levels became elevated, indicating the exercise was indeed strenuous.

The stress-related hormones cortisol and ACTH (adrenocorticotropic hormone) were analyzed in the blood samples. ACTH, elevated while on placebo, became significantly lowered by PS at the higher intake level (800 mg per day). PS also lowered the elevated cortisol: the 400 mg PS dose had an effect but failed to reach statistical significance, while the 800 mg dose caused a significant lowering of cortisol—to about 30 percent below the placebo levels.

This interesting outcome actually confirmed an earlier, similar double blind trial by Monteleone's group.[48] In that trial PS was administered by intravenous injection. Given by this route, PS also significantly blunted ACTH and cortisol release. It seems PS can be quite useful for down-regulating potentially harmful stress hormones.

PS Helps Avoid "Overtraining" During Workouts

A 1998 double blind trial done by Fahey and Pearl in the United States tackled the problem of overtraining in athletes.[49] Overtraining is an unhealthy imbalance between training and recovery, coming from too much training with too little time to recover. Overtraining is a well-known hazard of competitive sports. Athletes who overtrain can suffer decreased performance, injuries, depressed immunity, and psychological depression.

Measures that are relatively subjective, such as the subject's perception of well-being and muscle soreness, are often considered the most reliable markers of overtraining. In a complex "crossover" trial design, Fahey and Pearl gave PS as a dietary supplement (at 800 mg per day) to 11 fit male athletes doing intense weight training. The subjects would take either PS or placebo for two weeks, break ("wash out" the PS or placebo) for three weeks, then switch to the other for two more weeks. Blood samples were periodically collected and analyzed.

Elevations of the enzyme creatine kinase, an indicator of muscle damage, confirmed that the weight training regimen was indeed physically stressful for these subjects. But by the end of the trial, they had consistently reported markedly better well-being and lower index of muscle soreness while taking PS than while taking placebo. Another measure of benefit from PS was that every subject was able to guess correctly when he was taking PS as compared to when he was taking placebo. During the placebo phase subjects reported being virtually debilitated, but while on PS they were almost normal.

In summary, a total of five double blind trials were conducted with PS on mental and physical stress in young, healthy people. Two were done in the United Kingdom, two in Italy, the last in the United States. Altogether, they established that PS can soften both the negative psychological and physiological impact of stress in young, healthy people. So in addition to people who are aging or elderly, young people confronted with the stressful challenges of living in today's world may do well to supplement PS in their daily dietary regimen.

CHAPTER 7

PS For "ADD"— Excellent Early Results

- Being a very safe orthomolecule, PS is a valid brain nutrient for children.
- Preliminary observations by physicians indicate that PS may help children with attention, behavior and learning problems.
- PS and integrative medical management deserve further research as an alternative to the current drugging of children who have these problems.

PS appears to be very helpful for children with behavioral and attention problems, according to observations from preliminary clinical studies in which I had the privilege to participate. These are what they are—not double blind, simply what science calls pilot studies, probing for possible effects. Since PS occurs naturally in the body and is so safe to take, there was no problem to do such studies with kids. The results to date have been pleasantly surprising.

The research with PS on children actually was started by a grandmother who heard that it was useful for brain functions and very safe as a dietary supplement. She decided to give a little of it to her troublesome grandchild. At a health food show she searched me out and told me of her observations. She felt strongly that PS had helped her grandchild and urged me to explore this possibility for other children. Assertive grandmothers may be the best allies of problem kids—they don't stop until they achieve their goals.

The Kunin-Kidd Pilot Study[50,51]
In early 1997 I conferred with Richard Kunin, M.D., a pioneering nutritional psychiatrist now internationally renowned for his leadership in integrative medicine. After more than four decades of practice, Dr. Kunin is highly skilled at using dietary supplements to improve behavior and mental performance. He has made breakthroughs with both children and adults. Still, even for Dr. Kunin true cure of "ADD" kids had proved elusive. He graciously agreed to donate his time to try PS on kids with attentional and related behavioral problems. We ran a small ad in

the local newspapers, inviting parents to allow their children to participate in a pilot clinical study.

A few weeks later, we had five children and their parents in the doctor's waiting room. On this Saturday morning I was scared. These were the most unmanageable kids I had ever met! They had all come in at the same time, and they were all together in a pretty small space, looking to smash anything they could get their hands on. I found myself praying no one would get hurt.

After signing an Informed Consent form, the parents allowed their children to be evaluated by Dr. Kunin, with me in the office as his co-researcher. The doctor had designed a specific and detailed behavioral checklist for the parents to fill out on each child. The parents were asked to make an overall, "global" rating of their child's condition as compared with other children in his age range.

The doctor then did an attention span test (finger-tapping) and other skills assessments on each child, and took a detailed developmental and behavioral medical history. Each family unit received a supply of PS capsules sufficient for 200 mg PS daily (100 mg twice a day) for six weeks, and sent home. The study design required that no new vitamins or medications be prescribed except PS, and that no dietary changes be recommended.

The behavioral checklist rated 18 different types of behavior, each at four degrees of improvement needed to satisfy the parents' expectations: 0- normal; 1- slight improvement needed; 2- moderate improvement needed; and 3- much improvement needed, meaning clearly abnormal. On this scale a fully normal child should score 0, from no improvement needed per the parents' opinions. On the other hand, a highly abnormal child could score as high as 54, from needing much improvement on all 18 behavior measures.

When the children and their parents returned for evaluation, Dr. Kunin and I noticed the differences right away. Kids who before could not sit still were now playing happily in the office. One child dropped out—had failed to take the PS capsules on a regular basis. The remaining four kids did take the PS regularly, according to their parents. Three out of these four were significantly improved at the end of six weeks. The fourth was being passed back and forth between parents almost daily. He was considered improved by the mother, but the father did not report improvement. Let's briefly look at the three cases known for sure to be successful:

CASE 1. Began the study at age 4 years 6 months, healthy at birth but with speech development abnormally delayed. At the beginning his parents scored him at 37 of the possible 54 bad points. After being on PS for six weeks, his checklist score indicated marked improvement. The grandparents confirmed the parents' opinions, especially with regards to (a) boredom and lack of interest in general (b) patience and impulsiveness, (c) anxiety, overexcitement, destructive behavior, and ability to get along with other children. The doctor's examination confirmed remarkable improvements in his mood, cooperativeness, task performance, and attention span. Very unlike his first visit, in the doctor's office he was able to sit quietly and play while the adults were talking. His mother said: "This is the first time he has ever been able to play normally." Dr. Kunin noted: "I have never seen a child this badly off come around this much or this quickly."

CASE 2. Aged 5 years 3 months, already expelled from 10 schools and day care programs because of his oppositional and aggressive behavior. At school he required constant supervision to control his bullying and taking things from other children. He would attack other children without provocation, then when confronted by teachers he would kick, hit, head-butt and throw things. He had become anorexic and "zombie-like" in a trial on Ritalin, so had to be taken off that drug. At follow up after six weeks on PS, his improvement was unmistakable. His mother stated that "On his good days he is almost like a regular kid." For the first time he was able to attend a baseball game with his family, in contrast to previous times when they had to leave the game early due to his aggressive over-activity. After his course of PS he was accepted back into a day care program from which he had been expelled three months earlier, and was getting along well this time.

CASE 3. Aged 6 years 3 months, pleasant and cooperative but very distractible and complaining of poor memory. At school he got confused, sat in the wrong place, talked too much and screamed when frustrated. His drawing skills were highly deficient and he could not hold a memory well enough to repeat what he had just heard—a giveaway of neurologic damage. This boy had not used words until past two years old and did not form sentences until age three years. After PS, his behavioral checklist score was substantially improved. His most intense symptoms—restlessness and impulsive behavior—both improved; he was better able to focus attention and follow rules at school and also had improved at home. His anxiety and depression were improved, and he performed better in his tests at school and in his attitude toward the classroom.

In summary, the findings from this small pilot study indicate that PS (at 200 mg per day) seemed to markedly improve three out of four mentally disturbed children over the course of six weeks. No bad side effects of PS were noted. Dr. Kunin concluded, "This degree of improvement is similar to the benefits attributed to Ritalin®; however PS has no known adverse effects. On the face of it, it may be better for ADD than Ritalin."

The Ryser-Kidd ADHD Case Series
In early 1998 I was at a nutritional conference when this friendly person walked up to me and with a really pleasant demeanor, gently asked to talk with me about PS and kids. She was Carol Ann Ryser, M.D., a physician with a large practice in Kansas City that brings in a lot of kids with ADHD (attention deficit hyperactivity disorder, often called ADD). She wanted to investigate PS on some of her young patients. Soon we had developed a trial design and eventually recruited 27 children into this study, with the informed consent of their parents.

After assessing each child in-depth, Dr. Ryser developed an individual treatment plan for that child. Besides advising the parents and children (many of them teenagers) in behavioral management, she was highly experienced at prescribing dietary improvements and multiple nutrient supplements, and (yes, as necessary), pharmaceuticals. In our study, for each child she first set up her best program as per her usual practice, then later added PS into the treatment plans.

Dr. Ryser would prescribe PS at 200 or 300 mg per day, depending on the child's body size, then follow the child for at least four months. In the beginning she prescribed 100 or 200 mg per day, but soon she observed that by upping the daily intake, she could break through with the kids. Twenty-seven (27) children aged 3–19 years completed the study.

Dr. Ryser found that PS produced marked, clinically meaningful benefit for 25 of the 27 children. One child experienced partial benefit, and in one other no clear benefit was observed; it's not clear how compliant s/he was. PS improved attention, concentration, learning, and behavior, and benefited academic performance.

PS also consistently benefited the depression and anxiety commonly seen in these children. Some of the children did require a full four months to achieve a stable level of benefit from PS.

In children who were prescribed pharmaceuticals such as Ritalin (methylphenidate), Adderall (mixed amphetamines), or Wellbutrin (bupoprion), PS seemed to have additional clinical benefit. PS also extended the benefit experienced from nutritional supplementation with fish oil or primrose oil. No adverse effects or drug interactions were noted, consistent with PS's 20-year record of clinical use.

This apparent high degree of clinical benefit to children is consistent with the adult benefits from PS for memory conservation, brain revitalization, and stress management. These interesting findings suggest a need for further, more controlled research to establish just how much PS really can do to help kids. Society really needs alternatives for Ritalin and all the other drugs that sometimes hurt our kids.

Nutrients Are Safer Than Ritalin® for ADHD

As I worked with Dr. Ryser on my second study of PS for children, I was learning more about Ritalin (methylphenidate). Millions of children in the U.S. and other countries are being fed this potent methamphetamine-like drug. Though officially classified a narcotic, it is being prescribed for 70 percent of children diagnosed with ADHD (Attention Deficit/Hyperactivity Disorder). It acts on the brain with slower onset but almost identically to cocaine and amphetamines.

In my in-depth published review of ADHD, I listed some of the severe adverse side effects of Ritalin.[52] These include nervousness, agitation, anxiety, panic; paranoid delusions, psychosis, hallucinations; withdrawal, disorganization; aggressiveness, tendency to assault others. Also, findings that Ritalin caused cancer in mice generated considerable controversy. In a letter to the U.S. Government, the nonprofit Center for Science in the Public Interest (CSPI) said, "It is critical that a potentially carcinogenic drug (Ritalin) that is used by a large number of children over many months or even years be well tested and found to be appropriately safe…," Prominent cancer researchers and dietary experts have joined with CSPI to demand exploration of alternatives to Ritalin.

The use of Ritalin on kids is a highly questionable practice, especially since there is a safer and often more effective alternative. Total Health Management works for ADHD just as it works for everything else.[53] Of course, whenever a child is involved, it takes more than a little patience to sort out the factors that are switching the personality into the ADHD mode. Here also, as with other conditions, cooperation with an integrative healthcare practitioner can move the THM practice along.[52]

ADHD has multiple contributory factors—risk factors as for dementia. There is a genetic component to ADHD, but this on its own is not sufficient to trigger the symptoms. Adverse responses to foods and food additives are often involved as well as sensitivities to environmental chemicals, molds, and fungi. Exposures to toxins that damage the nervous system, such as the heavy metals mercury and lead and/or pollutant chemicals, are also suspected in ADHD. Even over-consumption of refined carbohydrates (sucrose and other simple sugars) can trigger ADHD–type symptoms in children.

Physicians with wholistic/integrative practices say that pretty much all the ADHD cases they see benefit to some degree when these factors are treated. Dr. Kunin, Dr. Ryser, Drs. Harding, Judah and Gant,[54] and many other integrative physicians are getting good to excellent results with ADHD children without having to use Ritalin. But the parents and the rest of society have to give them a chance to try the safe nutrients rather than starting with potentially harmful drugs.

The parent is indispensable for the total health management of ADHD. S/he can learn to identify whether their child is reacting to toxins at school or having adverse reactions to foods they get at home. They can monitor how much sugar their kids consume in the course of a day. In one large study it was found that 74 percent of hyperactive children studied had abnormal glucose tolerance.[55]

The THM strategy against ADHD means cleaning up the child's food, air, water, and school and home environment. One stirring and understandable, yet technically comprehensive source for help, is the book *Our Toxic World—A Wake Up Call*. This is the most recent of many informational works by Dr. Doris Rapp, the foremost physician expert on children's environmental sensitivities (see the RESOURCES section).[27]

Many nutrients can help with ADHD and the pilot clinical studies done to date seem to strongly suggest that PS is one of them. Another nutrient class likely to be helpful for ADHD is the omega-3 fatty acids. These are nutritionally synergistic with PS in the brain, as will be discussed in the next chapter.

CHAPTER 8

PS and DHA Amplify Each Other's Benefits

- The PS molecule is a "mother molecule" that also carries two fatty acids.

- PS carrying DHA omega-3 is a pivotal molecule for brain function. Cells of the healthy brain incorporate the two into their membranes as needed.

- Taking PS against a background of good DHA status is likely to be more beneficial than taking PS without having sufficient DHA in the body.

The double blind clinical trials and other human studies conducted with PS over the past three decades established its great value as a dietary supplement. Adding to this wealth of clinical knowledge on PS are the thousands of studies done with PS on laboratory animals, with cells in culture, even with isolated cell membranes and membrane proteins. These "basic science" studies are valuable to help us understand why PS is such a good dietary supplement. These studies also helped uncover a biochemical alliance between PS and another orthomolecular nutrient. This nutrient is the omega-3 fatty acid DHA (docosahexaenoic acid), which like PS works only in the cell membranes.

All cells have membranes. All the functions that keep cells alive rely heavily on the cell membrane systems. Cells rely on their membranes to make their life energy from nutrients, to use this energy to carry out their "housekeeping" life functions, and to manage their more sophisticated, specialized functions. Just about all the functions of life are based in

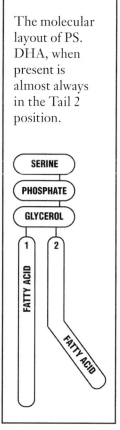

The molecular layout of PS. DHA, when present is almost always in the Tail 2 position.

SERINE

PHOSPHATE

GLYCEROL

1 2

FATTY ACID

FATTY ACID

or upon cell membranes, and PS is a universal building block for all cell membranes.

The simplest cells were little more than bags, with no nucleus or other internal structure and just one membrane holding some enzymes inside. This outer *cell membrane* separated the internal, living environment of the cell from the outer, nonliving environment that surrounded the cell. As cells became more advanced, the membrane expanded to include an internal network. A variety of specialized, membrane-bounded sub-compartments or "organelles" developed inside the cell. Each organelle has a microenvironment separately controlled by its own membrane system. The organelles are akin to specialized work stations, with the membranes being the work benches upon which the tools are mounted.

Nerve cells are no exception to this pattern. They have the usual variety of organelles, but their outer cell membranes are ultra-specialized to initiate and transmit their characteristic electrical and chemical signals. For this core function these cell membranes have ample amounts of PS and DHA built into them. This explains why the brain has more PS than do the other organs. The brain also has a lot of the body's DHA, much of it tied in with PS.

Two Overlapping Building Blocks for Cell Membranes
Cell membranes are made mostly from several different phospholipids, of which PS is just one. However PS has certain special ways of operating within the membranes. Some of its most valuable membrane activities make possible:

➡ **Transport Across the Membrane.**[56,57] The outer cell membrane that surrounds the cell carries a variety of transport proteins. These help control what molecules enter the cell and what molecules are allowed to leave. One such transporter controls the cell sodium to potassium ionic (charged) balance. This "sodium-potassium transporter" keeps so busy that it can use more than half of all the cell's energy. PS is closely associated with these molecules in the membrane, and is necessary for their activity. PS also helps support other transporters for calcium and magnesium.

➡ **Signal Transduction-Turning on the Cell.**[58] These are also located within the outer cell membrane. There are many different protein types that work together to transduce signals coming from outside the cell into molecular signals that penetrate the membrane. The protein kinases are a large family of proteins involved in memory formation, among their many functions. PS is required for their actions and for other signaling proteins as well.

➡ **Energy Generation.**[59] The mitochondria are the cell's energy factories. They churn out lots of ATP, the high-energy substance that is life's energy currency. Our cells depend on mitochondria for most of their energy. The mitochondria have highly active double-membrane systems that require a lot of PE (PhosphatidylEthanolamine, another phospholipid). PS is imported into the mitochondrial membranes as a prime source from which to make PE.

➡ **Nerve Transmitter Actions.**[60–63] The above functions of PS are operative in all our cells, but the brain is unique for its diverse chemical transmitter systems, almost all of which operate through cell membrane networks. PS is more abundant in those membranes that make, package, release, and respond to transmitters. Animal and "test tube" experiments prove that PS specifically supports the actions of acetylcholine, dopamine, adrenaline, noradrenaline, serotonin, GABA, endorphins, and other transmitters.

The head group of PS is specifically required for all these membrane actions of PS, but another dimension of PS action is to carry one particular fatty acid making up one or both of its tails. This fatty acid is the omega-3 DHA.

Omega-3 Fatty Acids, Important For the Entire Body

The long-chain omega-3 fatty acids EPA and DHA are vitamin-like nutrients that, like PS, are found in cell membranes. Like PS, they are building blocks for the membranes. Also similar to PS, they are key nutrients supporting fundamental cell functions. Most fascinating for our discussion is that they are intimately associated with each other in the membranes.

Both EPA (eicosapentaenoic acid) and DHA (docosahexaenoic acid) have been heavily researched and both are proven to be lifesaving dietary constituents. It is clearly confirmed that raising our dietary intakes of EPA and DHA dramatically reduces our risk for death from heart attack or other circulatory catastrophes, indeed against death from all causes.

The most omega-3 research has been done in the circulation field. The long-chain omega-3 duo EPA+DHA protects our blood vessels against inflammatory damage linked to coronary heart disease, heart attack, heart arrhythmia, and stroke. They also protect against arthritis, diabetes, inflammatory bowel diseases and inflammatory conditions in general. Evidence is accumulating that they may lower the risk for catastrophic memory decline. No doubt about it, EPA and DHA have lifesaving importance for the entire body.

On a practical basis our supplies of EPA and DHA have to come from the diet, either from the foods or from dietary supplements. Previously it was thought that humans could synthesize them from the shorter-chain ALA (alpha linolenic acid), but now it is clear that this process is very inefficient, if it can occur at all.[64] For all practical purposes, EPA and DHA are vitamins.

Human populations that cannot effectively make EPA or DHA from ALA include newborns, the aged, alcoholics, diabetics, hypertensives, the obese, or people with chronic viral infections. High blood cholesterol and high trans-fat intakes also are likely to interfere with the bio-transformation process, which happens on membranes. Healthy people actually have very little ALA in their cell membranes and it is unclear what role (if any) this omega-3 fatty acid has in human nutrition.

A study at the University of Edinburgh has been tracking people born back in 1936. Their mental performance was first tested in 1947. In 2001 their mental performance was again assessed and their red blood cells were analyzed for DHA+EPA content. Those who had the highest DHA+EPA in their red cells also showed the best performance on mental tests.

Though not conclusive, this finding suggests that higher omega-3 intakes could improve people's retention of their mental capacity as they age. A study in the Netherlands on middle-aged people came to a similar conclusion. With limited data currently available but more coming in, it seems dietary DHA+EPA can slow brain decline. This pattern of benefit from the omega-3s is mindful of the PS pattern.

Again in parallel with what we know about PS, DHA+EPA supplements can benefit mood control. Several double blind and other controlled trials indicate that they benefit clinical depression, manic depression (bipolar disorder), and ADHD and learning disorders in children.[41,52,53]

The membranes of human brain cells carry no detectable ALA, and no or very little EPA, but a substantial amount of DHA. This DHA normally is built into the structure of the PS molecules that help make these membranes. DHA is also incorporated into other phospholipids like PE (PhosphatidylEthanolamine) and PC (PhosphatidylCholine). But DHA's intimate functional synergy with PS is most clearly proven to support the higher brain functions.

DHA, The Omega-3, Very Important For Brain Cells

Beyond its general importance to all our cell membranes, DHA has extra special importance for cells of the brain. This longest of the long-chain omega-3s supports the growth and development of the fetal brain up to birth. Following birth there is a further high rate of brain growth, for which DHA is also important. The importance of DHA for the brain seems to continue all the way through to the end of life.

Much of DHA's action in the brain is wrapped up with PS molecules. DHA is found preferentially attached to PS as its tail 2. Since DHA has many double electron bonds (6), it has a great fluidizing effect in cell membranes. Having a DHA tail gives the PS molecule great fluidizing capacity. This has great functional implications because certain key proteins of the nerve cell membranes seem to require PS-DHA. One such is protein kinase C, a sophisticated protein and member of the large family of protein kinases that regulate membrane signal transduction.[65,66]

Protein kinase C is known to be crucial for initiating and consolidating memories. It must have PS and a highly fluidized membrane in order to work (interestingly, much of it is missing from Alzheimer's disease brain tissue). No wonder Dr. Norman Salem, the accomplished brain biochemist working at the U.S. National Institute for Mental Health, suggested, together with others of his team, that PS with DHA is one of the most important molecules for the brain.

PS and DHA Combine to Optimize Brain Function

PS-DHA is important for keeping the nerve cell membranes fluid, and no doubt for many other membrane functions as well. For the brain to have enough PS-DHA, two minimal conditions must be met. There must be enough PS available, and there must be enough DHA available to be combined with the PS molecules as the brain cells require.

One approach to ensuring these conditions are met could be to supply dietary PS pre-combined with DHA. Besides being technically very challenging to do, this approach has a built-in limitation: the tail will likely be chopped off before the PS molecule can reach the brain.

PS the nutrient is handled by the body much like any other dietary phospholipid. Before it can become absorbed it must pass through the stomach, where its digestion begins, then become further digested in the small intestine. The stomach's acid begins the process of cutting away the tail 2 of PS and the other phospholipids. Then enzymes in the intestine complete the tail 2 removal, for some 95 percent of the phospholipid molecules. PS and other altered phospholipid molecules are absorbed into the intestinal lining without a tail 2 attached (called "lyso" forms).

This proven pattern of PS digestion and absorption results in the intestinal lining cells stocking up on lyso PS. The DHA that is chopped away from position 2 can be moved somewhere else, even onto other phospholipids such as PE or PC. But the chances it will be recombined with the original PS molecule are virtually zero. The tail 2 profile of phospholipids is manipulated depending on the tissue where the molecule is present. Therefore PS in the blood has different tails from PS in the intestinal lining or PS in the brain. Functionally, this makes sense: Removing tail 2 prior to absorption gives the various tissues full flexibility to "assign" new tail 2s, depending on where the molecule will be needed.

Considering how the tissues handle DHA, what seems ultimately most important is that the whole body has enough DHA so that the brain (or retina, or testes) can draw on sufficiently ample supplies of DHA to tack onto PS (or PE, or PC), as needed.

Different zones of the brain have different PS tail 1 and tail 2 compositions. These seem to fulfill specific biochemical needs for that particular zone. Different PS molecules have differing effects on the membrane and different specific effects on the proteins in those membranes. In a variety of experiments conducted in the "test tube" setting and in laboratory animals, for certain membrane proteins phospholipids other than PS failed to do the job of PS. And the PS head group often worked best with DHA on position 2.

To summarize this section: the PS in our brain cells needs DHA, and the DHA needs PS. This is an example of biochemical synergy between two important orthomolecules. Both are fundamentally essential to the total performance of the brain. Both work best to help the brain when the other is fully available. To make them available, we have to generously supplement them in our diet.[67]

CHAPTER 9

PS For Total Health Management

- PS is a premier brain nutrient appropriate for long-term rebuilding of brain circuits.
- PS is best utilized together with daily practice—a lifestyle—of total health management.
- Ten practices of Total Health Management™ are listed and outlined.

The issue of safety cannot be taken for granted with dietary supplements. Supplements are generally not toxic the way pharmaceuticals often can be, but among supplements it is useful to distinguish xenobiotics (foreign) substances from ortho-molecular (intrinsic) substances. Consistent with its orthomolecular status in all known living things, PS is a very safe dietary supplement and is effective over a wide range of intakes. This, together with its marked benefits, makes PS a top priority as a foundational nutrient for Total Health Management practices.

PS is Safe to Take and Very Well Tolerated

The practical, clinical experience with PS for over two decades in Europe and North America indicates PS can be taken long-term without a problem. The longer experience with PS in laboratory animals and experimental "test tube" research leads to the same conclusion.

After extensive human and animal testing, PS is proven safe and non-allergenic. PS from soy (the usual commercial source) is well tolerated. Soy allergy (which is rare in the general population) does not seem to occur—since 1994 when soy PS was introduced into North America, not one case has come to my attention.

PS has been proven safe in standard animal toxicology tests. For example, several dogs were alive and healthy after being given PS by mouth at 70 grams per day for one year.[68] Out of the large number of human studies conducted with PS has come a flawless record of safety.

The decades of clinical observations on PS also indicate that it does not clash with common drugs. Clinical trials consistently report PS is compatible with pharmaceuticals commonly prescribed to the elderly. In their 1987 trial, Allegro and colleagues found PS had no clinically adverse interactions with drugs their patients were taking for high blood pressure, other cardiovascular problems, blood sugar control, diuretics, or chemotherapy.[69]

Also in 1987, Cenacchi's group reported on their laboratory findings from 130 subjects who took 300 mg of PS daily for up to 60 days.[68] They found no laboratory test abnormalities linked to PS. Subsequently, in 1993 they did a double blind trial with 300 mg PS per day for six months.[68] They allowed the elderly subjects to stay on their prescribed medications—antacids, anti-hypertensives, anti-inflammatories, antiulcer and mucolytic agents, diuretics, antithrombotics, hypoglycemics, antiarrthymics, insulin, calcium channel blockers, calcitonin and others. They could find no abnormal interactions with PS.

This 1993 Cenacchi trial also established that elderly patients (average age 77 plus) with chronic diseases could tolerate PS very well. This patient population in Italy had medical problems typical for their age group—cerebrovascular, artery and vein disorders, high blood pressure, heart disease, diabetes, lung diseases, digestive system diseases, arthritis. Only one PS patient dropped out from a side effect (dizziness) versus eight dropouts from the placebo group. Cenacchi's group stated, "These observations are remarkable…the large number of subjects enrolled in this study…represent a sample of the geriatric population commonly encountered in clinical practice."[34]

Such is the biological beauty of PS the orthomolecule. PS is so part and parcel of the normal workings of our cells that it is built into our biochemistry. Drugs conceivably could damage or deplete our membrane PS, but there is no indication or reason to expect that PS would do the opposite.

How to Take PS for Best Results

Being a "fat-soluble" nutrient and having to build up in the cell membranes, PS works best if taken at a high intake from the outset. Therefore I recommend 300 mg per day (taken with meals) for at least the first month. After that, depending on how much help is needed and how fast, 100 to 200 mg per day may be a reasonable maintenance intake.

Since PS is so safe, the more severe the person's problems, the more aggressive can be the supplementation strategy. Intakes up to

500 mg per day are proven effective and safe. For depression and anxiety I recommend a person start at 400 mg per day for a month or longer until s/he notices improvement in their mood. Then they can lower PS to the basal intake of 100 mg per day. *Tip*: DHA and EPA are also very helpful for mood.

People who prudently decide to take PS for a mental tune-up, or who choose to take one of the excellent combinations of PS with other nutrients, may find the 300 mg/100 mg schedule provides excellent results.

Since PS is so compatible with drugs and with other nutrients, people with challenging memory loss or other cognitive problems can simply add PS to all their other supplements and medications. One other nutrient they should be sure to take is DHA, which works so intimately together with PS in cell membranes.

Considering the crucial relationship between PS and DHA in the cell membranes, one has the best probability of getting benefit from PS if one is also getting at least 200 mg per day of DHA. This is best taken combined with at least 200 mg of EPA, in a roughly one-to-one ratio. These 200 mg daily intakes are the minimum intakes shown effective from the clinical research; most trials used higher intakes. It's highly likely that the more EPA+DHA over 200 mg that is taken daily, the faster they will build up in the cell membranes to work in synergy with PS.

For people who have been clinically diagnosed with a memory or mood disorder, I strongly recommend finding a healthcare professional committed to the integrative practice of medicine. Put simply, integrative practitioners do all they can to help their patients, treating the patient as a whole human being and putting nontoxic therapies (such as nutrients) first.

Having an integrative practitioner on your team helps balance against pro-drug, anti-nutrient prejudice from the mainstream. Amazingly, some mainstream physicians still advise their patients to stop taking all vitamins. Trying to do your own self-management with only a conventional provider (the 10-minute visit) can be frustrating, ineffective, and sometimes downright dangerous to your health.

Integrative physicians know of PS and use it in their practice. The great body of clinical findings on PS, combined with its exceptional safety record, motivates these physicians to use PS as the core of their brain vitality protocols. People of all ages can benefit from PS. Taking PS and DHA is helpful to optimize the brain's many functions, to help restore functions that are out of balance, and to slow the functional decline that comes with the passing of the years.

Total Health Management Will Amplify PS Benefits
Many of us alive today want to be empowered about our health. We want to stay free of disease, believe that we can always better our health (the concept of optimal health), are scared to death of being in a hospital. We pursue the Holy Grail of long life without illness. Those of us who are working the hardest at this are practicing Total Health Management. THM is, in my opinion, the best and only insurance against a decrepit and pain-ridden life.

Practicing THM means training ourselves to do good things for our health, each and every day. This doesn't mean we "can't eat anything, because the media says it's all bad for us." Nor does it mean "I can't ever have fun because I'm stuck with this stupid diet." Simply, practicing THM means living our daily life with greater consciousness and understanding of what's at stake if we do something or if we don't.

Practicing THM also helps us avoid being misled by fatalistic watercooler talk about "bad" genes. The scientific fact is, our genes have meaning and power only in the context of the environment in which they are made to function. With the full human genome now known, science is clear on this point: Unhealthy personal lifestyle, the deterioration of the modern food supply, and the polluted planetary environment, all contribute far more to our risks for catastrophic decline of brain and body than do any of our genes.

There's one hitch to practicing THM: it takes commitment and work. You need to really do it. This is not something someone else can do for you, not your spouse or your doctor or your therapist. You have to be willing to listen to your body, to make a commitment to staying healthy—a commitment to eating wisely, exercising regularly, meditating, getting enough sleep, thinking clearly, cultivating good judgment in personal relationships. You can't have clear thought processes without having a healthy head on a healthy body. The Top Ten Practices of THM follow on the next page.

The Top Ten Practices of Total Health Management
To do your best to avoid dementia, and to help everything else about your health to improve, master for yourself the following 10 daily practices:

1. Avoid Toxic Agents. Cigarette smoke, active or passive; excessive alcohol consumption (including beer and wine); mercury from dental fillings, vaccines, factory emissions; other heavy metals like lead, cadmium, arsenic; polluted water; pesticides, herbicides, fungicides; junk food with rancid fats and additives; all the known risk factors for dementia.

2. Use Your Brain, or Risk Losing It. Extensive animal experimentation has shown that the more the brain is stimulated, the more stem cells get to work building new circuits. "Plastic" remodeling of established circuits follows very similar principles. Therefore take courses, play word games, card games, other games of concentration. Read good books (too much TV can cause the brain to deteriorate). Memorize telephone numbers, rather than relying on automatic dialers. If you've suffered major memory loss, purchase one of the reputable memory training programs and use it every day.

3. Get Regular Physical Exercise. This increases blood flow to the brain and simultaneously helps the other organs. In the animal experiments just mentioned, the stem cells worked even better when the animals had a treadmill for physical exercise. Work out hard enough to break a sweat, for at least half an hour at least five times a week.

4. Get Rid of Emotional Stress. This is a sadly underrated brain killer. If you have any doubt about how damaging emotional stress can be, read Dr. Robert Sapolsky's classic paperback *Why Zebras Don't Get Ulcers*. Sometimes taking care of this problem means making hard decisions to change jobs or modify personal relationships. Don't worry, these can be upgraded to better jobs and better personal relationships.

5. Take Care of Your Blood Sugar. Many life stressors, whether emotional or chemical in origin, lower blood sugar. This is particularly dangerous to the brain, which uses a big chunk of the body's blood sugar while at rest and even more while concentrating and doing mental tasks. Brain cells need an ongoing, smooth supply of blood glucose, and when deprived will begin to die off within minutes.

6. **Eat Sensibly and Regularly,** to keep the brain tissue continually supplied with the glucose and nutrients it needs. Keep fried foods to a minimum, because frying generates harmful free radicals. The brain's high content of omega-3s and other unsaturated fats makes it particularly vulnerable to free radicals. Help guard against free radical attack by cooking with spices rich in antioxidants, such as garlic, onions, ginger, curry, rosemary. Berries make a great antioxidant dessert.

7. **Be Careful of Food Additives.** Some are likely "excitotoxins" that can drive nerve cells into a death frenzy. Glutamate, as in MSG (monosodium glutamate); and aspartate, as in Aspartame, fall into this category. Artificial colorants are mostly suspect carcinogens. Trans-fats ("hydrogenated fats") are hidden in many foods and are linked to chronic disease. Try to stay with fresh foods, minimally processed and packaged. Spend more on organic foods.

8. **Drug Habits are No Good.** ALL the illegal drugs, and many of the legally available pharmaceutical drugs, are brain toxins. Cocaine, amphetamines, Ecstasy and other psychedelics, all kill brain cells. So can marijuana. Some pharmaceuticals are as toxic to the brain as the illegal drugs. This is another medical scandal waiting to happen.

Many drugs currently in wide use as sleep aids, as antidepressants, or for other indications, can have profound negative effects on the brain. Drugs such as Librium, Valium, Halcion, Prozac, Haldol, Xanax, Compazine, Stelazine, Thorazine and barbiturates are responsible for an estimated 10 percent of all cases that present as dementia. Those patients fortunate enough to be taken off the drug will sometimes recover their minds.

Some of these drugs also are linked to homicidal and suicidal behavior. Sadly, many physicians prescribe drugs without being familiar with their side effects. It's up to the consumer to beware. Again, *Worst Pills, Best Pills* is an indispensable resource for this type of information.

9. **Develop Your Personal Dietary Supplement Program.** Even the most conservative physicians and scientists who are honest now agree that dietary supplements are essential for good health. Partly this is because of the lousy state of the food supply. Also, the emotional and physical stressors of modern living increase our metabolic needs for nutrients. Then as we get older (past 30, that is) we digest, absorb, and assimilate our foods with less efficiency. My article, *"Developing a Personal Vitamin Program,"* originally published in *totalhealth* magazine, will help you set up your own program (see the RESOURCES section for how to contact *totalhealth* magazine). My Web site has many other articles on various disorders and diseases, and nutritional protocols for each. PS is mandatory for memory, learning, mood, and stress management.

10. **Take Time to Sleep.** This could be the most neglected part of modern life. The body needs seven to eight hours of sleep to renew all the tissues, including those of the brain. The brain's pineal and pituitary glands keep the body on a 24-hour schedule, synchronized according to sleep patterns. When sleep is incomplete, these sophisticated hormonal cycles become disrupted, resulting in accelerated aging and greater susceptibility to disease.

CHAPTER 10

PS Does Something For Everyone

- You don't have to lose your mind as you age. Revitalize your brain with PS.
- Everyone, including young people and even children, very likely stands to benefit from PS.
- To hesitate is to lose—get started on PS and total health management as soon as you can.

Despite all the nervous jokes people make about it, severe memory loss and other mental decline is not inevitable with advancing age. Many people become centenarians and remain mentally sharp, but so much of modern Western living contributes to accelerated wear and tear on the brain. Taking PS, DHA, multivitamin-minerals, and antioxidants helps us conserve our brain circuits, to make it through life without losing our minds. One aging musician said something like, "If I'da known I was gonna live this long, I would've taken better care of myself."

PS Really Can Revitalize the Brain

The many clinical trials done with PS clearly prove it has the potential to "turn back the clock" on brain decline. It also seems able to help some younger people. PS as a dietary supplement makes valuable contributions to the brain vitality of people, whatever their age. But PS is not a panacea—it has to be started before the brain is too far gone, while there are still circuits to work with.

PS is a very useful single nutrient for improving brain function, but it will work better in conjunction with a comprehensive personal brain improvement program. And it will work best when the Top Ten Practices of THM are followed with reasonable discipline.

Altogether, the findings from more than a hundred human research studies, and thousands of other studies, support the conclusion that PS benefits just about every brain function that can be tested. These benefits go from boosting glucose consumption by the aging brain, to enhancing nerve cell receptors for growth

67

factors and nerve transmitters to stimulating membrane signal transduction functions for memory consolidation. But PS even goes a step further. In animal experiments PS protects against the usual loss of nerve cell size seen in aging rats, and PS seems to facilitate

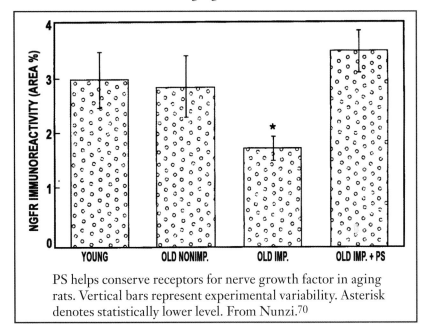

PS helps conserve receptors for nerve growth factor in aging rats. Vertical bars represent experimental variability. Asterisk denotes statistically lower level. From Nunzi.[70]

the action of nerve growth factor, one of the brain's natural agents for boosting stem cell maturation.

PS probably has a trophic, or growth support effect, on the tissues of the brain. Further animal experiments were combined with "test tube" biochemical experiments to show that PS conserves the membrane receptor proteins that sense nerve growth factors. These are small molecules that permeate the brain and stimulate circuit renewal, probably partly through increasing stem cell participation. Interestingly, these work better when the brain is more stimulated.

The illustration shows that as rats age, their brain nerve cells tend to lose nerve growth factor receptors and with them, the capacity to respond to NGF. Some rats lose more than others, and also perform worse on "intelligence tests"—these are the Old Impaired Group (rather like a demented group). Giving PS to these rats as they age boosts their NGF receptor density to a level roughly equivalent to young rats. This is a very important experiment because it clearly suggests PS is having a rejuvenating effect on the rat brain. There's no obvious reason why it should not do the same for the human brain and thereby support stem cell maturation in our needy brains.

In the future, research breakthroughs with stem cells may succeed to reverse AAMI, ARCD, MCI, possibly even dementia itself. But for those individuals who right now are concerned about the state of their brains, waiting is not going to help. The drugs currently licensed for dementia offer very limited benefits. Therefore taking PS, DHA, and other essential vitamins and minerals, and making the dietary-lifestyle and the other total health management changes I've outlined, are the only real options for avoiding further memory decline and the risk of descending into dementia.

Taking a Stand for Dementia Prevention: Dr. Dharma
Dharma Singh Khalsa, M.D., is internationally recognized as a leader in body/mind medicine. Along with his other distinguished training, he studied mind/body medicine at Harvard, medical acupuncture at UCLA, and researched pain management at the University of California San Francisco Medical Center. Charismatic, open minded, and intelligent, he is highly skilled in all the principles of Total Health Management. He actually pioneered many of them. In 1993 he founded the Alzheimer's Prevention Foundation International (APFI) currently located in Tucson, Arizona.

At the APFI clinic, a wide range of services are offered within a structured integrative approach to rebuilding the damaged brain. APFI speaks of "Four Pillars of Prevention"— diet and vitamins, stress management, exercise and brain aerobics, and pharmaceuticals. The latter are used with caution, and include hormone replacement therapy as appropriate. Dr. Dharma is very strong on stress management techniques such as meditation, guided imagery and visualization, hypnosis, deep breathing, music, massage, and prayer. His yoga meditation techniques were found by SPECT scanning to improve attention, concentration, and short-term memory. The changes in the scans from before to after were consistent with better judgment, improved psychological health and enhanced spiritual activity.

"Dr. Dharma" as he is affectionately known, has written several groundbreaking books all highly relevant to Total Health Management. Among them are *Brain Longevity*, published in 1997 and now translated into 12 languages. *Meditation as Medicine*

(2001) received great critical acclaim. *Food as Medicine* (2003) and *The Better Memory Kit* (2004) are both loaded with hands-on, user friendly tips for improving memory through diet, lifestyle, and overall total health management.

The work of this medical pioneer stands as a beacon to those (including myself) who are convinced that accelerated memory decline can be slowed and probably halted by the use of PS and other nutrients and practicing Total Health Management. The extensive services of the APFI (see the RESOURCES section) are available to individuals who are confronted by out of control memory decline. We try to help ourselves as far as we can get results, but when a situation gets out of control, it's best to seek a professional. If the situation can be turned around, Dr. Dharma is one to help you do it.

PS Can Benefit Other Brain Conditions
PS also can be helpful for brain problems not directly related to memory loss. Take Parkinson's disease, for example. In a 1987 exploratory open trial by Fuenfgeld and Nedwidek in Germany,[71] 12 Parkinson's patients were given PS in doses ranging from 200 to 500 mg per day for three weeks. Eight (8) of the 12 showed substantial motor improvement. Three weeks was the minimum period required to see benefit and very likely a longer dosing period would have produced benefit in more of the subjects.

The apparent benefits of PS for Parkinson's patients in this small pilot study are supported by findings from animal experiments. PS was found to elevate dopamine in the brains of aging rats and boosted their nerve cell membrane receptors for dopamine.[72]

PhosphatidylSerine has the potential to help with the abnormal brain seizures experienced by epileptics. In 1987, Loeb and co-researchers administered PS to human subjects suffering from sporadic seizure abnormalities, for periods ranging from 30 to 90 days.[73] They gave PS in combination with GABA (gamma aminobutyric acid), a nerve transmitter known to have calming effects.

The combination of PS plus GABA worked against absence seizures in the epileptic subjects. One-third of the subjects experienced a greater than 50 percent reduction of this seizure type. In 1989, from doing experiments with rats, Loeb's group found that the calming effect on seizure activity was achieved only by combining GABA with PS and not with PC or other phospholipid.[6]

Cocito and collaborators later did a related human trial that might have been designed to fail. They gave a single dose of PS to patients with seizures and found it did not work very well.[74] This is not at all surprising, of course. PS is a fat-soluble nutrient and so would require at least several days (preferably several weeks) of daily dosing to build up in the nerve cell membranes and eventually produce a clinical benefit.

It may be worthwhile for clinicians to do a longer term trial of PS together with GABA, in epileptics. A well-designed trial with substantial doses of both these nutrients would likely help advance the total health management of epilepsy.

Parting Message: Everyone May Benefit from PS

Contrary to some popular assertions about this incredible nutrient, it does not become depleted from the brain as we get older. Nor is PS technically a vitamin, because no PS deficiency state has been described. But PS resembles the vitamins more so than herbal preparations—it is orthomolecular, it has highly predictable benefits, and it is safe to take and very well tolerated.

PS doesn't just help the brain. Typical for an orthomolecule, PS supports a diverse range of pro-homeostatic processes throughout the tissues:

★ PS is a reservoir for phospholipids to build mitochondria, the energy factories of our cells. This means PS is important for energy generation throughout the body.

★ PS is an important component of the normal blood coagulation process.

★ PS in the outer membrane helps all cells receive and respond to important external stimuli, by the process called signal transduction.

★ PS facilitates cell-to-cell signaling.

★ PS is essential for the disposal of dead and dying cells by the immune system. Prompt disposal of cells that can no longer survive helps to cut down the potential for autoimmune or inflammatory damage.

★ PS provides support for a great variety of life functions, both by way of its linkages with DHA and by its general presence in all our cell membranes.

PS (PhosphatidylSerine)

PS may well be a conditionally essential nutrient and maybe it's harder for our cells to make from scratch as we age. This happens for lots of orthomolecules. But this also doesn't explain why PS can improve quality of life for young healthy people as well as for older people. The preliminary findings that suggest PS helps children adds to its allure for the young and healthy, as well as for the old.

Lots of dietary supplement products are available that claim to improve brain function. None has the track record of PS. Herbal extracts can be beneficial, but perhaps because they are not orthomolecular, they do not measure up to PS. Its orthomolecular status gives PS such great potency and safety that it can be comfortably put to long-term use. This feature of PS is important because the brain's task of mobilizing growth factors, growing out new nerve cells, and reorganizing circuits probably takes years. PS from a reputable supplier can be taken daily by the consumer for as long as it takes to get the benefits s/he seeks.

In summary, whatever the extent of a person's mental challenges, whatever his level of emotional stress, no matter how anxious or depressed he is, he is likely to get some benefit from taking PS, especially as part of a Total Health Management plan. I encourage my readers to get a professional brain assessment and give a copy of this book to your healthcare provider.

What is at stake here, no more and no less, is avoiding dementia. All of us know that dementia is a personal and family catastrophe that also places an incalculable emotional and financial burden on society. Dementia has no cure, but there is evidence that the progressive memory loss that comes before dementia at least can be slowed by PS, particularly if total health management is also upgraded. The key is to start early, preferably at the first signs of memory loss, well before it becomes so severe that it interferes with the individual's quality of life.

Whether or not you, Dear Reader, believe you have any kind of brain problem, I offer my sincere professional opinion that you will benefit from a brain conservation program tailored to your needs. PS should be at the core of your brain conservation and revitalization program. By taking PS and practicing the Top Ten Principles of Total Health Management, you can reasonably expect your brain power will improve. There's no time to lose: the earlier you and the people you love can get started, the better.

PS Double Blind Trials For Memory

Trials Against Age-Associated Memory Impairment

1. Crook and collaborators, USA and Italy.[17] T. H. Crook and five co-researchers did this multicenter U.S. trial with 149 patients who fit the criteria for age-associated memory impairment (AAMI). Their findings were published in 1991 in the journal *Neurology*. The details of their methods and results are covered in Chapter 2, so are not duplicated here.

2. Jorissen and others, Netherlands.[75] One double blind trial with PS was disappointing. This was the trial conducted in the Netherlands by Jorissen and collaborators. The researchers concluded PS had no benefit in the trial. Dr. Tom Crook kindly agreed to comment on the design of this trial.[76] He found that the tests used were inappropriate for the type of human subjects used in the trial. This was supposed to be a trial on subjects with AAMI, yet the tests were not sensitive to AAMI. Here's an excerpt from Dr. Crook's critique:

> The choice of tests is a matter of greater importance in that an appropriate test should meet specific criteria, principal among which are that it must clearly relate to the clinical problems the subject is experiencing and that it must be "valid." Validity is the most important feature of any psychological test and means the test measures what it purports to measure. Specifically, in the case of later-life memory impairment, a valid test must relate clearly to the memory problems people experience in everyday life and must be sensitive to the clear linear decline that occurs with advancing age. That is, people in their 30s should perform at a higher level than people in their 40s and so on. Also, among older people, the test must distinguish between those with quite modest clinical problems and those whose problems are more severe.

> In our studies, all tests used to measure PS effects were shown in nearly 100 scientific publications to be relevant to the problems of older people and to fulfill the other necessary criteria for validity. We tested many thousands of people around the world and showed repeatedly that test performance declines markedly, and in a linear manner through the adult years. We also showed that the tests clearly distinguish between older persons with modest clinical problems and those whose problems are more severe. By contrast, there is clear evidence that many of the tests used by Jorissen and his colleagues to assess the effects of PS were invalid. The tests were all abstract and had no apparent relation to the problems experienced by older individuals in everyday life and, beyond

that, many were not sensitive to the decline in memory that occurs with advancing age. How, for example, can a test be used to assess the effects of a compound on Age-Associated Memory Impairment if older people perform as well as young people on the test and, even among older people, those with serious memory problems do as well as those with modest problems?

Thomas Crook, Ph.D., personal communication to Dr. Parris Kidd, 2002.

Trials Against Alzheimer's Dementia

1. Delwaide, Belgium.[32] P. J. Delwaide and three co-researchers did this trial at the University of Liege in Belgium, and published their results in 1986. The patients were 35 hospitalized men and women, aged 65 to 91, all with mild to moderate memory and other cognitive loss characteristic of Alzheimer's. The patients were randomly assigned to two groups, the PS group to receive PS at 300 mg per day (with meals) and the placebo group.

The patients were evaluated at baseline, then after one week and six weeks of dosing, and once more at three weeks past the end of dosing. Rating scales were used to make clinical evaluations. The Crichton Rating Scale scored orientation, communication, cooperation, agitation, mobility and mood, as well as bowel control, dressing, feeding and sleep patterns. The Peri Scale was also used—developed by Delwaide and others; it was a 49-point, more sensitive scale than the Crichton. Also used was the Circle Crossing Test, a test to pick circles out from other geometric forms.

The PS group improved over placebo on all three of these measures and on the Pen Scale the improvement reached statistical significance. When the 49 items of the Peri Scale were grouped into 10 categories, PS was linked to improvement in all 10. PS was particularly superior to placebo in the categories of toilet, dressing, feeding, bowel control, bladder control, ability to go to the toilet unaided, and verbal expression. The authors noted a degree of improvement from PS that could be useful for subjects and their families.

2. Amaducci, Italy.[33] In 1988, Amaducci's group published another well-designed double blind trial with PS on Alzheimer's. This Italian Multicenter Study of Dementia involved 22 researchers working in seven Italian neurology research centers. The 115 patients, ages 40 to 80 (average age 62), were randomized into two groups, a PS group that received 200 mg per day and a placebo group. The dosing period was three months, with follow-up at six months.

Benefits from PS were not significantly different from placebo by the end of dosing (at three months). However, benefits were more evident at six months (three months after dosing with PS ended). This could suggest that the relatively low dose of PS that was used (200 mg per day) took longer than three months to have its full effect. By the six-month stage, those patients who began the trial with more severe impairment were the subgroup that derived significantly more benefit from PS over placebo. Three months after the severely afflicted subgroup ceased to receive PS, their scores on "personal memory," "overall memory" (using the Blessed Dementia Scale) and on performance of everyday activities were significantly improved.

The experienced Italian dementia researchers who conducted this study concluded from their findings that PS does slow or prevent further cognitive deterioration in persons with established dementia. Particularly noteworthy from this study was that the benefits of PS could still "break through" clinically at three months after the patients were taken off of it.

3. Fuenfgeld and others, Germany.[5] In 1989, Fuenfgeld's group at the University of Marburg and the Schlossberg Klinik Wittgenstein did a double blind trial on Parkinson's disease patients with dementia of the Alzheimer type. They selected 62 patients who had dementia symptoms but also abnormal slowing on the EEG (ElectroEncephaloGram). Over 21 days, half received a placebo, the other half received PS at 300 mg per day. At that point the EEGs were repeated. It was found that the brain zones with previously slow EEG had been speeded up by PS, towards a healthier pattern. Some 70 percent of the PS subjects showed this improvement.

Clinically, after just 21 days, the PS group overall was significantly less depressed and less anxious, and had more motivation than did the placebo group. This was especially true for those patients who had more severe motor problems related to a longer time with Parkinson's. These clinicians did other studies with individual patients and concluded that 500 mg PS per day sometimes produced more substantial improvement. Intravenous injection of PS (50 mg per day) gave further benefit in some cases.

4. Hershkowitz and others, Israel.[77] In Israel in 1989, Dr. Moshe Hershkowitz and three co-researchers did a small double blind trial. Fifty-two (52) Alzheimer's patients were randomly divided into two groups, one of which received placebo for six months while the other received PS (300 mg). PS was found to improve significantly the measure Orientation in Time.

In household management and daily activity, there were clear statistical trends but not sufficient to warrant a judgment in favor of PS. This statistical inadequacy my be related to the relatively small sizes of the patient groups. After two years of follow-up of these patients, it was determined that patients who had taken PS were less likely to have become non-cooperative or to be institutionalized. The researchers suggested that had their patient groups been larger, they would have found a wider range of improvements from PS.

5. Crook, USA.[18] In 1992, Dr. Thomas Crook and co-researchers from Vanderbilt University and Italy published their double blind, randomized trial on Alzheimer's patients. Fifty-one patients were studied whose ages ranged from 55 to 85 (average age 71 years). The PS group received 300 mg PS daily for 12 weeks, the other group got a placebo. Assessments occurred at baseline, then at three, six, nine and 12 weeks.

By week 12, the end of the dosing period, the PS-treated subjects showed the following four types of improvements (statistically significant at p<0.05):

1. Memory for names of familiar persons, clinic staff members, for example.
2. Recall of the locations of frequently misplaced objects.
3. Recall of details of events from the previous day.
4. Recall of details of events from within the past week.

These improvements were not especially impressive, but a subgroup of patients who started the trial with relatively mild cognitive impairment derived additional benefits from PS. This mildly demented subgroup benefited on the four tests listed above, as well as on three others:

5. Ability to maintain concentration.
6. Lessened inclination to complain of memory deterioration.
7. Far less apparent memory impairment in a clinical interview.

The benefits of taking PS were apparent as early as three weeks after the beginning of dosing. Crook and colleagues concluded that PS had a mild therapeutic effect in patients who had not progressed to the middle and later stages of the disorder.

6. Engel and others, Germany.[78] Conducted by Dr. Rolf Engel and seven collaborators at the Psychiatric Hospital of the University of Munich. This was a small trial, conducted with 33 patients with mild primary degenerative dementia of the Alzheimer type. PhosphatidylSerine (200 mg per day) was compared against placebo.

This double blind trial was also a crossover trial: patients were first given either PS or placebo for eight weeks, then "washed out" with no treatment for eight weeks, after which the treatments were reversed for another eight weeks. Clinical global improvement ratings showed significantly more patients improving while on PS than while on placebo. Findings from EEG mapping indicated that PS overall shifted the EEG pattern more towards the normal level.

7. Cenacchi, Italy.[34] Conducted by Dr. Teresa Cenacchi and her collaborators, this GERMIS (Geriatric Multicenter Italian Study) is the largest trial published to date on PS for Alzheimer's. It involved 425 subjects of ages 65 to 93 (average age 77+ years), recruited at 23 institutions in northern Italy and coordinated by a large number of investigators. All the subjects had moderate to severe cognitive decline; very severely affected Alzheimer's patients were excluded.

The patients were given PS at 300 mg per day, or a placebo, for six months. They were assessed at baseline, then at three months after dosing began and again at six months. After statistical analysis, the memory and learning scores on a verbal recall test were significantly improved in favor of PS. The scores on withdrawal and apathy also indicated significant improvement for the PS group. PS significantly improved motivation, initiative, interest in the environment, and socialization. The investigators concluded, "The resulting improvements in adaptability to the environment can have an important impact on the quality of life of such patients."

This Cenacchi trial confirmed the optimistic results obtained with PS in the previous trials. It also made a unique and needed contribution to the clinical experience with PS by establishing that patients taking commonly prescribed pharmaceutical drugs still tolerate PS well. The investigators searched thoroughly for PS-pharmaceutical interactions, and for any adverse effects from PS, and found none.

Trials Against Non-Alzheimer's Dementia
1. Palmieri, Italy.[79] In 1987, C. Palmieri and R. Palmieri and their co-researchers published the results of their double blind trial. This trial was carried out simultaneously at three research centers in Italy. It involved 87 subjects with "moderate" cognitive deterioration of a degree corresponding to clinical dementia. The subjects' ages ranged from 55 to 80 (average 73.1 years). After randomization and baseline evaluations, PS was given at a 300 mg daily dose in comparison with placebo, and the evaluation repeated at 60 days. PS was then discontinued, and a follow-up evaluation was done 30 days after PS dosing was withdrawn.

In this trial, the PS group benefited on tests of attention, concentration and short-term memory. On the five-word memory test, the improvement of the PS group was very impressive. On the broader clinical assessment, PS improved activities related to daily living, and especially seemed to lessen the apathy and withdrawal to which people with cognitive problems are often found susceptible. Items that were statistically improved included self-sufficiency in activities of daily living; sleep disturbances; abnormal behavior; initiative; and the overall behavioral deficit, which was highly significantly improved.

The authors stated, "PhosphatidylSerine appears to exert an action in two distinct contexts: one relating to the cognitive effects of vigilance, attention, and short-term memory, and the other relating to behavioral aspects such as apathy, withdrawal and daily living. . . ." (p. 81).

2. Nerozzi, Italy.[80] D. Nerozzi and collaborators published in 1987 the results of another double blind trial conducted in Italy. This one involved 35 subjects, 60 to 80 years of age, recruited from retirement homes near Rome. The degree of cognitive loss again resembled clinical dementia and approximated that of the patients in the Palmieri trial. Here also, the PS group received 300 mg daily versus the placebo group, and the trial ran for 60 days. The PS group experienced statistically meaningful benefit on delayed memory recollection.

3. Ransmayr and others, Austria.[81] G. Ransmayr and three colleagues did this double blind trial with 39 patients, all of them elderly and having brain circulation problems (chronic cerebrovascular disease) as well as evidence of cerebral arteriosclerosis. Half the patients received 300 mg PS per day, and half received placebo, for two months. No significant changes were found using old-line psychometric tests. However, flicker-fusion frequency (FFF) data showed a significant improvement in the PS group of patients.

The FFF test is a measure of the brain's physiological efficiency at sensing flickering light, but the brain's levels of vigilance, concentration, and motor factors also contribute to its results. Further statistical analysis indicated that the improvement of FFF by PS was superior to that by the placebo.

4. Villardita, Italy.[82] This was another multicenter trial. Published in 1987, it involved 170 subjects, ages 55 to 80 (average age 65.7), with mild to moderate cognitive deterioration. The PS group received 300 mg daily versus the placebo group, and the trial ran for 90 days.

By the end of this trial, 12 of the 24 tests reached statistical significance in favor of PS. Tests for attention and vigilance were all highly significant, as were the tests of word manipulations linked to memory. PS also significantly improved performance on both immediate and delayed memory tests. Villardita and collaborators concluded that PS benefits attention and alertness in subjects with more advanced memory decline. They suggested that if taken at earlier stages of decline prior to dementia, PS would likely save those cognitive processes that are often the first to go as dementia develops.[8]

Resources

Alzheimer's Association (U.S.) Web site, www.alz.org. Authoritative source of statistics on Alzheimer's and other dementias, with information also on pharmaceuticals approved or under investigation.

Alzheimer's Prevention Foundation International, Tucson, Arizona, www.alzheimersprevention.org, tel 520-749-8374. Founded by Dharma S. Khalsa, M.D. a visionary physician trained at the University of California San Francisco, Harvard and other elite medical institutions. This is the most comprehensive program available for reversing mental decline.

Amen, D.G., M.D. *Images of Human Behavior.* A Brain SPECT Atlas. Newport Beach, California: MindWorks Press, 2003. A dazzling collection of images of healthy, damaged, or diseased brains obtained via metabolic SPECT imaging in the clinics of Daniel Amen, M.D. A must-see for the serious brain student or parent of a troubled child. www.mindworkspress.com.

Crook, T, Adderly, B. *PS, The Memory Cure.* New York:Pocket Books, 1998. Dr. Tom Crook, world expert on cognition testing and age-associated memory impairment, co-wrote this very good book. In it he presents a 6-step plan for sharpening mental skills.

Khalsa, D.S., M.D. and Stauth, C. *Brain Longevity: The Breakthrough Medical Program.* New York: Pocket Books, 2001. Now a classic in the field. Available from Alzheimer's Prevention Foundation, www.alzheimersprevention.org, tel 520-749-8374.

Khalsa, D.S., M.D. and Stauth, C. *Meditation as Medicine.* New York: Pocket Books, 2001. Another pioneering work by this cutting-edge brain healer. Barnes and Noble health book of the year. Alzheimer's Prevention Foundation International, www.alzheimersprevention.org, tel 520-749-8374.

Khalsa, D.S., M.D. *Food as Medicine,* 2003. Alzheimer's Prevention Foundation International, www.alzheimersprevention.org, tel 520-749-8374.

Khalsa, D.S., M.D. *The Better Memory Kit,* 2004. Alzheimer's Prevention Foundation International, www.alzheimersprevention.org, tel 520-749-8374.

Kidd, Parris, PhD. Web site, www.dockidd.com. Wide array of articles for lay people, scientists and physicians on the integrative management of memory decline, ADHD, autism, bipolar disorder, Parkinson's, multiple sclerosis, and other brain disorders. Also many readable articles on why to take vitamins, dangers posed by pollutants, benefits of PS and other brain nutrients, and other columns originally published in *totalhealth* magazine.

Passwater, Richard, PhD. www.drpasswater.com
Nutrition pioneer, prolific scientific author, contributor to the development and application of dietary supplements for more than 3 decades. His Web site lists his 40 books and much more.

Perlmutter, David, M.D. Web site, www.BrainRecovery.com.
Brilliant integrative physician tackling the most difficult to treat brain conditions. His now classic book *BrainRecovery.com* is indispensable for its informational content and treatment protocols. His more recent *The Better Brain Book* (authored with Carol Colman) expands on his earlier protocols and includes newer diagnostic tests and cooking recipes.

Phospholipid Educational Web site, www.phospholipidsonline.com
Covering phospholipid types and applications, with the participation of Dr. Parris Kidd.

Rapp, Doris, M.D., www.drrapp.com.
A physician who has dedicated her career to identifying and eliminating toxic influences on the human environment from foods and pollutants. Her latest book, *Our Toxic World: A Wake-Up Call,* should be in the home of every family.

Ryser, Carol Ann, M.D., www.carolannreysermd.net.
Health Centers of America, Kansas City, Missouri.

totalhealth **magazine,** published by Total Health Communications, St. George, Utah, tel 435-673-1789, www.totalhealthmagazine.com. The nation's foremost magazine promoting citizen empowerment in health management.

U.S. Food and Drug Administration (FDA) Center for Food Safety and Applied Nutrition, www.cfsan.fda.gov.
Communications, analysis, and exact text with updates, of approved qualified health claims for PS.

U.S. National Institutes of Mental Health (NIMH), www.nimh.nih gov/health information. Conservative but responsible source for information on ADHD, autism, bipolar disorder, major depression, and other mental illness.

Worst Pills, Best Pills II, www.citizen.org/publications published by Dr. Sidney Wolfe and the Public Citizen Health Research Group, Washington, DC.; An honest, uncorrupted reference for pharmaceuticals in common use or recently developed for use. Encyclopedic yet affordable, a must reference for every household.

References Cited in the Text

1. Total Health Publications/Science&Ingredients Inc. Protected Trademark: Total Health Management™ USA; 2005.
2. Science and Ingredients Inc. Protected Trademark: Vital Lipid™ USA; 2005.
3. Folch J. The chemical structure of phosphatidylserine. Journal of Biological Chemistry 1948;174:439–50.
4. U.S. National Library of Medicine, PubMed. Comprehensive database of peer-reviewed scientific and clinical journals. www.ncbi.nlm.nih.gov/entrez; 2005.
5. Fuenfgeld EW, Baggen M, Nedwidek P, others. Double blind study with phosphatidyl serine (PS) in parkinsonian patients with senile dementia of Alzheimer's type (SDAT). In, Alzheimer's Disease and Related Disorders (Progress in Clinical and Biological Research 317); 1989, 1235–46.
6. Loeb C. Antiepileptic activity of GABA and phosphatidylserine. In, Phospholipids in the Nervous System: Biochemical and Molecular Pathology, ed. Bazan NG, Horrocks LA, Toffano G. Padova: Liviana Press;1989, 93–100.
7. Klinkhammer P, Szelies B, Heiss WD, others. Effect of phosphatidyserine on cerebral glucose metabolism in Alzheimer's disease. Dementia 1990;1:197–201.
8. Kidd PM. The phospholipids as anti-aging nutraceuticals. In, Anti-Aging Medical Therapeutics—Volume IV, ed. Klatz RM and Goldman R. Chicago, IL: American Academy of Anti-Aging Medicine;2000, 282–95.
9. U.S. Food and Drug Administration. Center for Food Safety and Applied Nutrition/ Office of Nutritional Products and Dietary Supplements. Phosphatidylserine and cognitive dysfunction and dementia (qualified health claim: final decision letter). May 13, 2003; www.cfsan.fda.gov.
10. Alberts B, Johnson A, Lewis J, others. Molecular Biology of the Cell. New York: Garland/Taylor and Francis;2002.
11. Crook TH. Diagnosis and treatment of memory loss in older patients who are not demented. In, Treatment and Care in Old Age Psychiatry, ed. Levy R, Howard R, Burns A. Hampshire, UK: Wrightson Biomedical Publishing;1993, 95–111.
12. Crook TH, Adderly B. The Memory Cure. New York: Simon and Shuster;1998.
13. totalhealth magazine, pioneering Total Health Management. St. George, Utah, USA; www.totalhealthmagazine.com;2005.
14. Goldman WP, Morris JC. Evidence that age-associated memory impairment is not a normal variant of aging. Alzheimer Disease and Associated Disorders 2002;15:72–9.
15. Ritchie K, others. Classification criteria for mild cognitive impairment. American Academy of Neurology 2001;56:37–42.
16. Petersen RC, others. Current concepts in mild cognitive impairment. Archives of Neurology 2001;58:1985–992.
17. Crook TH, Tinklenberg J, Yesavage J, others. Effects of phosphatidyserine in age-associated memory impairment. Neurology 1991;41:644-9.
18. Crook T, Petrie W, Wells C, others. Effects of phosphatidylserine in Alzheimer's disease. Psychopharmacology Bulletin 1992;28:61–66.
19. Sinforiani E, Agostinis C, Merlo P, others. Cognitive decline in ageing brain: therapeutic approach with phosphatidylserine. Clinical Trials Journal 1987;24:115–24.
20. Pauling L. Orthomolecular psychiatry. Science 1968;160:265–71.
21. Alzheimer Association (U.S.). Dementia statistics. www.alzorg; 2005.
22. Amen DG. Images of Human Behavior. A Brain SPECT Atlas. Newport Beach, California: MindWorks Press;2003.
23. Kidd PM. A review of nutrients and botanicals in the integrative management of cognitive dysfunction. Alternative Medicine Review 1999;4:144–61.
24. Khalsa DS. Brain Longevity: How to Regenerate Your Mind for Peak Mental Performance. New York: Warner Books;1997.

PS (PhosphatidylSerine)

25. Khalsa DS, Stauth C. Meditation as Medicine: Activate the Power of Your Natural Healing Force. New York: Pocket Books;2001.
26. Tierney MC, Szalai JP, Snow WG, others. A prospective study of the clinical utility of ApoE genotype in the prediction of outcome in patients with memory impairment. Neurology 1996;46:149–54.
27. Rapp DJ. Our Toxic World. Buffalo, N.Y.: Environmental Medicine Research Foundation; 2004.
28. Wolfe SM. Worst Pills, Best Pills II. Washington DC: Public Citizen Health Research Group;1993.
29. Lupien S, de Leon M, de Santi S, others. Cortisol levels during human aging predict hippocampal atrophy and memory deficits. Nature Neuroscience 1998;1:69–73.
30. Sapolsky RM. Why Zebras Don't Get Ulcers: A Guide to Stress, Stress-Related Diseases, and Coping. New York: W.H. Freeman;1994.
31. Geula C, Mesulam MM. Cortical cholinergic fibers in aging and Alzheimer's disease: a morphometric study. Neuroscience 1989;33:469–81.
32. Delwaide PJ, Gyselynck-Mambourg AM, Hurlet A, others. Double blind randomized controlled study of phosphatidylserine in demented patients. Acta Neurologica Scandinavica 1986;73:136-140.
33. Amaducci L, the SMID Group. Phosphatidylserine in the treatment of Alzheimer's disease: results of a multicenter study. Psychopharmacology Bulletin 1988;24:130-134.
34. Cenacchi T, Bertoldin T, Farina C, others. Cognitive decline in the elderly: A double blind, placebo-controlled multicenter study on efficacy of phosphatidylserine administration. Aging (Clinical and Experimental Research) 1993;5:123–33.
35. Sengupta N, Datta SC, Sengupta D. Platelet and erythrocyte membrane lipid and phospholipid patterns in different types of mental patients. Biochemical Medicine 1981;25:267–75.
36. Rabboni M, Maggioni FS, Giannelli A, others. Neuendocrine and behavioural effects of phosphatidylserine in elderly patients with abiotrophic or vascular dementia or mild depression. Clinical Trials Journal 1990;27:230–40.
37. Gindin J, Novikov M, Kedar D, others. The effect of plant phosphatidylserine on age associated memory impairment and mood in the functioning elderly. Geriatric Institute for Education and Research and Department of Geriatrics, Kaplan Hospital, Rehovot, Israel; 1995, 10–25.
38. Manfredi M, Pranteda G, Sacca A, others. Risultati clinici della fosfatidil-serina in 40 donne affette da turbe psico-organiche, in eta climaterica e senile. [Clinical results of phosphatidylserine in 40 women affected by psycho-organic disturbances, in menopausal and senile conditions]. La Clinica Terapeutica 1987;120:33–36.
39. Maggioni M, Picotti GB, Bondiolotti GP, others. Effects of phosphatidylserine therapy in geriatric patients with depressive disorders. Acta Psychiatria Scandinavia 1990;81:265–70.
40. Brambilla F, Maggioni M, Panerai AE. B-Endorphin concentration in peripheral blood mononuclear cells of elderly depressed patients effects of phosphatidylserine therapy. Neuropsychobiology 1996;34:18–21.
41. Kidd PM. Bipolar disorder as cell membrane dysfunction. Progress towards integrative management. Alternative Medicine Review 2004;9(2):107–35.
42. Selye H. The Stress of Life (Revised). New York: McGraw-Hill;1976.
43. Benton D, Donohue RT, Sillance B, others. The influence of phosphatidylserine supplementation on mood and heart rate when faced with an acute stressor. Nutritional Neuroscience 2001;4:169–78.
44. Nerozzi D, Magnani A, Sforza V, others. Early cortisol escape phenomenon reversed by phosphatidylserine (Bros*) in elderly normal subjects. Clinical Trials Journal 1989;26:33–8.
45. Masturzo P, Murialdo G, de Palma D, others. TSH circadian secretions in aged men and effect of phosphatidylserine treatment. Chronobiologia 1990;17:267–74.
46. Benton D. Phosphoglycerides for use in improving heart rate recovery. Privileged communication; 2001.
47. Monteleone P, Maj M, Beinat L, others. Blunting by chronic phosphatidylserine administration of the stress-induced activation of the hypothalamo-pituitary-adrenal axis in healthy men. European Journal of Clinical Pharmacology 1992;41:385–8.

References

48. Monteleone P, Beinat L, Tanzillo C, others. Effects of phosphatidylserine on the neuroendocrine response to physical stress in humans. Neuroendocrinology 1990;52:243–8.

49. Fahey TD, Pearl MS. The hormonal and perceptive effects of phosphatidylserine administration during two weeks of resistive exercise-induced overtraining. Biology of Sport 1998;15:135–44.

50. Kunin RA. PS for ADD: Better than Ritalin. The New Fillmore (San Francisco, California, USA);1998.

51. Kunin RA, Kidd P. Pilot study of phosphatidylserine (PS) in young children with attentional and behavioral abnormalities. Unpublished results;1998.

52. Kidd PM. Attention Deficit/Hyperactivity Disorder (ADHD) in children: rationale for its integrative management. Alternative Medicine Review 2000;5(5):402–28.

53. Kidd PM. ADHD total health management, the safe and effective alternative to Ritalin. totalhealth magazine (St. George, Utah, USA);2000.

54. Harding KL, Judah RD, Gant C E. Outcome-based comparison of Ritalin® versus food supplement-treated children with AD/HD. Alternative Medicine Review 2003;8:319–30.

55. Whalley LJ, Fox HC, Wahle KW, others. Cognitive aging, childhood intelligence, and the use of food supplements. American Journal of Clinical Nutrition 2005;81(6):1453–54.

56. Suzuki S, Yamatoya H, Sakai M, others. Oral administration of soybean lecithin tran phosphatidylated phosphatidylserine improves memory impairment in aged rats. Journal of Nutrition 2001;131:2951–56.

57. Carafoli E. Biogenesis: Plasma membrane calcium ATPase, 15 years of work on the purified enzyme. FASEB Journal 1994;8:993-1002.

58. Mosior M, Epand RM. Mechanism of activation of protein kinase C: Roles of diolein and phosphatidylserine. Biochemistry 1993;32:66–75.

59. Shiao YJ, Lupo G, Vance JE. Evidence that phosphatidylserine is imported into mitochondria via a mitochondria-associated membrane and that the majority of mitochondrial phosphatidylethanolamine is derived from decarboxylation of phosphatidylserine. Journal of Biological Chemistry 1995;270:11190–98.

60. Gelbmann CM, Mueller W E. Chronic treatment with phosphatidyserine restores muscarinic cholinergic deficits in the aged mouse brain. Neurobiology of Aging 1991;13:45–50.

61. Cohen SA, Mueller W E. Age-related alterations of NMDA-receptor properties in the mouse forebrain: partial restoration by chronic phosphatidylserine treatment. Brain Research 1992;584:174–80.

62. Gagne J, Giguere C, Tocco G, others. Effect of phosphatidylserine on the binding properties of glutamate receptors in brain sections from adult and neonatal rats. Brain Research 1996;740:337–45.

63. Moynagh PN, Williams DC. Stabilization of the peripheral-type benzodiazepine acceptor by specific phospholipids. Biochemical Pharmacology 1992;43:1939–45.

64. Su HM, Bernardo L. Dietary 18:3n-3 and 22:6n-3 as sources of 22:6n-3 accretion in neonatal baboon brain and associated organs. Lipids 1999;34 (Supplement):S347–S350.

65. Newton AC, Keranen LM. Phosphatidyl-L-serine is necessary for protein kinase C's high-affinity interaction with diacylglycerol-containing membranes. Biochemistry 1994;33(21):6651–8.

66. Newton AC, Johnson J E. Protein kinase C: a paradigm for regulation of protein function by two membrane-targeting modules. Biochimica et Biophysica Acta 1998;1376:155–72.

67. Kalminjn S, others. Dietary intake of fatty acids and fish in relation to cognitive performance at middle age. Neurology 2004;62:275–80.

68. Cenacchi T, Baggio C, Palin E. Human tolerability of oral phosphatidylserine assessed through laboratory examinations. Clinical Trials Journal 1987;24:125–30.

69. Allegro L, Favaretto V, Ziliotto G. Oral phosphatidylserine in elderly patients with cognitive deterioration. Clinical Trials Journal 1987;24:104-108.

70. Nunzi MG, Milan F, Guidolin E, others. Therapeutic properties of phosphatidylserine in the aging brain. In, Phospholipids: Biochemical, Pharmaceutical, and Analytical Considerations, ed. Hanin I and Pepeu G. New York: Plenum Press;1990, 213–18.

71. Feunfgeld EW, Nedwidek P. Neurohomologous phosphatidylserine in parkinsonian patients with associated disorders of cerebral metabolism. Clinical Trials Journal 1987;24:42–61.

72. Calderini G, Bellini F, Bonetti AC, others. Pharmacological properties of phosphatidylserine in the ageing brain. Clinical Trials Journal 1987;24:9–17.

73. Loeb C, Benassi E, Bo G, others. Preliminary evaluation of the effect of GABA and phosphatidylserine in epileptic patients. Epilepsy Research 1987;1:209–12.

74. Cocito L, Bianchetti A, Bossi L, others. GABA and phosphatidylserine in human photosensitivity: a pilot study. Epilepsy Research 1994;17(1):49–53.

75. Jorissen BL, Brouns F, van Boxtel MPJ, others. The influence of soy-derived phosphatidylserine on cognition in age-associated memory impairment. Nutritional Neuroscience 2001;4:121–34.

76. Crook TH. Critique of the Jorissen et al 2001 trial. Personal communication; 2002.

77. Hershkowitz M, Fisher M, Bobrov D, others. 1. Long-term treatment of dementia Alzheimer type with phosphatidylserine: effect on cognitive functioning and performance in daily life. In, Phospholipids in the Nervous System: Biochemical and Molecular Pathology, ed. Bazan NG, Horrocks LA, Toffano G. Padova: Liviana Press; 1989, 279–88.

78. Engel RR, Satzger W, Guenther W, others. Double blind cross-over study of phosphatidylserine vs. placebo in patients with early dementia of the Alzheimer type. European Neuropsychopharmacology 1992;2:149–55.

79. Palmieri G, Palmieri R, Inzoli MR, others. Double blind controlled trial of phosphatidylserine in patients with senile mental deterioration. Clinical Trials Journal 1987;24:73–83.

80. Nerozzi D, Aceti F, Mella E, others. Fosfatidilserina e disturbi della memoria nell'anziano [Phosphatidylserine and impaired memory in the elderly]. La Clinica Terapeutica 1987;120:399–404.

81. Ransmayr G, Plörer S, Gerstenbrand F, others. Double blind placebo-controlled trial of phosphatidylserine in elderly patients with arteriosclerotic encephalopathy. Clinical Trials Journal 1987;24:62–72.

82. Villardita C, Grioli S, Salmeri G, others. Multicentre clinical trial of brain phosphatidylserine in elderly patients with intellectural deterioration. Clinical Trials Journal 1987;24:84–93.